THE MELODY OF FAITH

THE MELODY OF FAITH

Theology in an Orthodox Key

VIGEN GUROIAN

William B. Eerdmans Publishing Company

Grand Rapids, Michigan / Cambridge, U.K.

© 2010 Vigen Guroian
All rights reserved

Published 2010 by
Wm. B. Eerdmans Publishing Co.
2140 Oak Industrial Drive N.E., Grand Rapids, Michigan 49505 /
P.O. Box 163, Cambridge CB3 9PU U.K.
www.eerdmans.com
Printed in the United States of America

15 14 13 12 11 10   7 6 5 4 3 2 1

Library of Congress Cataloging-in-Publication Data

Guroian, Vigen.
The melody of faith: theology in an Orthodox key / Vigen Guroian.
p.   cm.
ISBN 978-0-8028-6496-3 (pbk.: alk. paper)
1. Orthodox Eastern Church — Doctrines.
2. Theology, Doctrinal — Popular works.   I. Title.

BX320.3.G87   2010
230′.19 — dc22
                                          2010000135

Four of the chapters in the book are retitled and revised versions
of previously published articles:

"Salvation: Divine Therapy." *Theology Today* 61, no. 3 (October 2004): 309-21.

"Mother of God, Mother of Holiness: A Meditation." In *Holiness: Past and Present*, ed. Stephen C. Barton (London/New York: T&T Clark, 2003), chapter 16, pp. 339-57.

"I Confess the Cross Because I Know of the Resurrection." *St. Vladimir's Theological Quarterly* 50, no. 4 (2006): 339-55.

"O Death, Where Is Your Sting?" *Sin, Death, and the Devil*, ed. Carl E. Braaten and Robert W. Jenson (Grand Rapids: Wm. B. Eerdmans, 2000), pp. 118-31.

For

Nathan A. Scott Jr. (1925-2006)
in gratitude for his enduring friendship

CONTENTS

ACKNOWLEDGMENTS ix

PREFACE xi

1. The Litany of Creation 1

2. The Luminous Moment of the Apocalypse 25

3. Divine Therapy 43

4. Mother of God, Mother of Holiness 65

5. The Victorious Cross 93

6. The Rhythm of the Resurrection 115

NOTES 137

SUBJECT INDEX 153

SCRIPTURE INDEX 156

ACKNOWLEDGMENTS

This book is dedicated to Nathan A. Scott Jr. of blessed memory. I could not have imagined, when I arrived at the Religious Studies Department of the University of Virginia in 1978 to spend the first three years of my academic career there, that a black man my father's age would take such a special, personal interest in me. Nathan's confidence in my potential and his constant encouragement gave me inspiration and the courage to push on. During more than twenty-five years of friendship and correspondence, until his death in 2006, Nathan unfailingly read my work; he read every one of my books. He embraced me as a peer, and he also made me feel like a son in the radiance of a father's pride. I will never forget his gift of love.

There are other persons and organizations to which I owe a debt of gratitude for the completion of this book. I especially thank Howard and Roberta Ahmanson for making possible the inclusion of the color plates in this book. Also, through the Fieldstead Foundation, they enabled me to take a much-needed leave for the academic year 2005-2006, during which I completed several chapters of *The Melody of*

Acknowledgments

Faith. For their support, which continues even into the present, I am profoundly grateful. Likewise, I wish to thank the Earhart Foundation for the grant that allowed me to complete Chapter 1 and revise other chapters during the spring and summer of 2008.

I am indebted to Mary Hietbrink at Eerdmans, whose fine editorial instincts have been a great help, and whose patience and attentiveness have made everything so much easier. Last, it has been my exceptional good fortune to discover Carrie Frederick Frost at the University of Virginia. I have directed Carrie's master's thesis, and she, in turn, with her sharp editing skills and theological insight, has been of invaluable assistance to me.

PREFACE

Fifteen years ago, after he had read a draft of my book *Life's Living Toward Dying,* Jon Pott, editor-in-chief at William B. Eerdmans Publishing Company, commented to me, "Vigen, you write tone poems." If that be true, and I believe that Jon was on to something, then perhaps it is no accident that the title of this book is *The Melody of Faith.* The six chapters that comprise this book do not constitute a systematic account of the Christian faith in the Germanic style of rational academic theology. Its coherence and organization are less architectonic than musical. This is consistent with the general character of Orthodox Christian theology. Orthodox theology is, for the most part, occasional and topical, though there are significant exceptions.

This sextet of theological "tone poems" does not progress in a linear or "rational" fashion. Instead, a melody builds in which central beliefs of the Christian faith appear and reappear, variously expressed. In music, a melody is created by a set or sequence of melodic phrases, each of which expresses an "idea" or "theme." Repetition and variation of these phrases contribute to the melody and enrich it. Something

Preface

similar happens here. Thus, for example, while Creation is the special subject of Chapter One, the chapters that follow develop the rich, multivalent meaning that Creation has in Christian belief and practice. The same may be said of sin, forgiveness, redemption, and salvation.

I am, of course, speaking metaphorically. The Christian faith is not literally a melody or song. Nevertheless, the musical metaphor is especially appropriate to theology. It may be that theology is nearer in origin and character to music than to architecture, despite modern assumptions to the contrary. It is generally understood that music and religion are primordially related to one another, that, in fact, one almost inevitably finds music where human beings practice religion. In primitive culture, music is inherently religious, expressing basic beliefs about beginnings and endings as it is employed in worship of deity. Music originates at the wellspring of human emotions[1] and expresses an experience of the numinous.

Great voices of the Christian faith have spoken of an extra-sensory (or trans-sensory) musicality of Creation. In his tract *Religio Medici*, Sir Thomas Browne, that winsome wise man of the late Renaissance, mused that there is something of divinity even in "vulgar and Tavern-Musick." "More than the ear discovers," Browne opined, music "is an Hieroglyphical and shadowed lesson of the whole World, and creatures of God. . . . It is a sensible fit of that harmony which intellectually sounds in the ears of God."[2]

It is not my purpose here, however, to reflect at length on the relation of music to religion. I want to be more specific. Within the history of Christianity, it certainly is the case

Preface

that before the rise of Christian art and architecture there was music. The Gospels and letters of St. Paul testify to this, as well as writings of the first- and second-century Christian apologists. In Matthew's Gospel we read that after the disciples supped in the Upper Room, "they . . . sang a hymn" and "went out to the Mount of Olives" (Matt. 26:30, NKJV). In his letter to the Ephesians, St. Paul exhorts, ". . . be filled with the Spirit, speaking to one another in psalms and hymns and spiritual songs, singing and making melody in your heart to the Lord" (Eph. 5:18-20, NKJV). Writing in the second century, Justin Martyr observes, "We offer thanks by invocations and hymns for our creation."[3] And Eusebius of Caesarea quotes Caius (also known as Gaius), a presbyter in the church at Rome at the beginning of the third century: "For who is ignorant of the books of Irenaeus and Melito, and the rest, which declare Christ to be God and man? All the psalms, too, and hymns of brethren, which have been written from the beginning by the faithful, celebrate Christ the Word of God, ascribing divinity to Him."[4]

One thing more needs to be said here about music. Not one of the passages I have cited uses the Greek word for music. In primitive and ancient culture, music includes much more than the specific art form that we identify as such. Melody itself has a broader application than in scientific musicology. Its etymology refers us back to poetry and song. Primitive and ancient culture does not distinguish music from poetry, as we are in the habit of doing. Are the Psalms or the hymns of the fourth-century Syriac poet and theologian St. Ephrem the Syrian music or poetry? The simple answer is that they are both.

Preface

The hymnody that I cite and employ as resource for the theology in these pages *is* poetry. Vocalization, syllabic inflection, and such are far more significant than harmonization or orchestration. Indeed, traditionally, this hymnody within its liturgical settings has not included instrumental accompaniment. The presence of the organ in some Orthodox churches today, particularly in Western Europe and North America, is a late development.

This is significant. It points to the primacy of words rather than notes or chords. Words also form images, especially when we speak of poetry. And in a liturgical setting this may take on heightened significance. Theology that is done in an Orthodox key will represent and reflect this synergy of word and image in the liturgy. Though I have titled this little volume *The Melody of Faith,* I might have called it *Images of Faith.* In these essays, I include the imagery not only of Orthodox hymnody but also of Orthodox iconography and Gospel illumination.

In *The Sacred in Life and Art,* Orthodox theologian Philip Sherrard writes that the icon properly belongs within "a framework of belief and worship." It is part of a larger visual system of the church structure that acts synergistically with Scripture and hymnody to convey and support "the spiritual facts or spiritual events that underlie the whole drama of... [the] liturgy."[5]

An icon is not just a picture. Image and picture are not the very same thing in either art or poetry. The icon does not seek to replicate nature but presents a transfigured Creation returned to its original harmony and symphonic unity. It is nearer in spirit to poetry than to plastic art. The entire

Preface

ensemble of icons in Orthodox Christianity composes a cosmos. The contemporary Orthodox theologian Andrew Louth writes that this cosmos "embraces the invisible and the visible; ... the material and the spiritual; ... is reflected in the inner reality of the human being; ... moves from creation to consummation by way of the paschal mystery of Christ; ... [and] is the communion of saints of both the Old and New Testaments."[6] In Orthodox liturgy, Scripture, hymnody, and iconography together chorus the melody of faith.

To this chorus, I have added my own voice. On occasion, I recall personal experiences in which images of faith have come alive for me. Through song and the veneration of icons, gestures of bowing, prostration, signing of the cross, and tasting of the supper, each and every person who participates in the liturgy becomes a liturgist, a consecrator and transformer of this profaned world into sacred reality. The same may be said of doing theology.

An ancient hymn, one of several score collected in a hymnal of the first or second century known as the *Odes of Solomon*, likens the five senses to the strings of a harp through which "the Spirit of the Lord speaks."[7] This seems right, so that we justifiably broaden the meaning of melody beyond the auditory to include sight, smell, taste, and touch also, since God in Christ has redeemed and sanctified us whole, in body, mind, and soul. That is certainly the conviction from which, and the spirit in which, I have written this book.

A confession is in order before closing. My title is a barely disguised borrowing from another book. In 1998, Jaroslav Pelikan published *The Melody of Theology*, a dictionary of

PREFACE

theological and philosophical terms. In the preface, Pelikan explains that he wrote *The Melody of Theology* in answer to an invitation from a friend at Harvard University Press "to prepare a book that 'could amount to a kind of autobiography in small bites — for it has the beguiling simplicity of being organized by the alphabet. . . . [A] kind of *summa* of [one's] work and life.'" But even Pelikan borrowed his title from Nicephorus of Constantinople, who in the ninth century described the Trisagion of the Byzantine Liturgy as a "thrice-illumined melody of faith."[8]

In the summer of 2000, at a beach on the New Jersey shore, I read *The Journals of Father Alexander Schmemann: 1973-1983*. I marked an entry for Thursday, April 5, 1973, in which Schmemann wrote: "At the hour of death, what will remain of life is a unique vision of an unchanging altar, an eternal gesture, a continuous melody. There is really nothing better; truly a revelation."[9] I hope that in some small way this book serves to confirm in my reader's mind and heart the profound truth of Father Schmemann's observation.

CHAPTER 1

The Litany of Creation

In the immense cathedral which is the universe of God, each man, whether scholar or manual laborer, is called to act as the priest of his whole life — to take all that is human, and to turn it into an offering and a hymn of glory.

Paul Evdokimov,
Woman and the Salvation of the World

A year ago, one cool September morning, I set off for the Blue Ridge, not far from my home in Culpeper, Virginia, to meet my grown daughter, Victoria, at Old Rag Mountain. We hiked the eight-mile circuit up to the top of the mountain, scaled the jagged stone outcropping for which Old Rag is well-known, and descended to the verdant river valley on the mountain's northeast side. The trek took the better part of a day, and we came down from Old Rag as the sun was setting.

The last leg of the circuit leads on to a broad fire road that equestrians use. As we looked over to Old Rag on our right, we watched the late afternoon light retreat into shadows. Darkness descended on the dense deciduous forest as the sun sank behind the mountain. The contours of the ridge were drawn dramatically, like the vaulting of a great cathedral. Victoria and I were gripped with awe and appreciation for the beauty and sheer grandeur of these surroundings. We commented to one another that no human artifice could compare to what nature — nay, God — had laid before us. The songbirds were in chorus and seemed to voice our thanksgiving. And we agreed that what we were experiencing at that moment was truly a gift of faith. "Prayer," says John of Kronstadt, "is a state of continual gratitude."[1] What lay before us might quite naturally evoke gratitude in the human heart, but to whom do people without a belief in God express their gratitude? "To whom will he [man] be thankful, to whom will he sing the hymn . . . without God[?],"[2] asks Dmitri Karamazov of *The Brothers Karamazov*.

My thoughts turned to the book of Genesis. From the opening verses of Genesis through to the books of Psalms and the Prophets, the Old Testament envisions the whole of Creation, heaven and earth, as a vast temple in which the people gather in liturgy to give praise and honor to the Maker and thank him for the beauty and goodness of his Creation. God lays the foundations (Ps. 104:5), sets up the pillars (1 Sam. 2:8), stretches out the canopy (Isa. 40:22), and frames the windows (Mal. 3:10). He is enthroned within the temple, as heavenly and earthly choirs glorify his name.

The first chapter of Genesis introduces the awe-inspiring mystery that Creation springs from a divine litany of which God is both celebrant and respondent, so that the liturgy of

The Litany of Creation

Creation is truly a divine liturgy in which we may participate and sing "Amen":

> God said, "Let there be light"; and there was light. *And God saw that the light was good.* . . . And God said, "Let the waters under the heavens be gathered together . . . and let the dry land appear." And it was so. . . . *And God saw that it was good.* . . . And God said, "Let the earth bring forth living creatures according to their kinds. . . ." And God made the beasts of the earth according to their kinds. . . . *And God saw that it was good.* (Gen. 1:3-4, 9-10, 24-25, RSV)

Ancient Israel not only envisioned Creation as God's temple, but also built its houses of worship as microcosms of the universe. The Hebrew temple incorporated symbols of all the elements and forces of the cosmos. The temple on Mount Zion in Jerusalem "holds down the forces of chaos and sustains the first action of creation," says Douglas Knight. "Zion is the foundation, cornerstone, and navel"[3] of the world. The sacrifice and the smoke of incense symbolize God's presence. God meets humanity in the temple, as heaven and earth are there united.

Hymnody and song fill and finish the temple. Indeed, in a real sense, hymnody "builds" the temple. The Hebrew Scripture is replete with music, especially in the great treasure chest of the Psalter. Its songs for voice, sometimes for instrument also, belong to the temple and are as vital to it as the stones with which it is constructed. The liturgy of Creation continues in the temple. God's people are its voice: "I will sing to the Lord as long as I live; I will sing praise to my God while I have my being" (Ps. 104:33, RSV).

In the Darkness something was happening at last. A voice had begun to sing. . . . One moment there had been nothing but darkness; the next a thousand, thousand points of light. . . .
C. S. Lewis, *The Magician's Nephew*

No one who has read C. S. Lewis's Narnia books can forget the scene early in *The Magician's Nephew* in which the lordly lion Aslan sings the Narnian world into existence. With his marvelous literary invention, Lewis captures a truth about God and Creation of which theologians who build systems of doctrine often lose sight: that Creation is not only harmonious but musical, and not *just* musical, either, but a sacred music, a hymnody. The poet hears this melody and sings it out:

> . . . Heark! In what Rings
> And *Hymning Circulations* the quick world
> Awakes and sings!
> The rising winds,
> And falling springs,
> Birds, beasts, all things
> Adore him in their kinds.
> Thus all is hurl'd

The Litany of Creation

In sacred *Hymnes* and *Order,* the great *Chime*
And *symphony* of nature. Prayer is
The world in tune,
A spirit-voyce,
And vocall joyes,
Whose *Eccho* is heav'ns blisse.

Thus writes the seventeenth-century Welsh poet Henry Vaughan in his poem *The Morning-watch.*

In his *Inscriptions on the Psalms,* St. Gregory of Nyssa of the fourth century muses that the whole cosmos "is a kind of musical harmony whose musician is God."[4] In a sensory world of time and space, we experience the temple and the song as separate and distinct. Even so, we can gain a sense of how in eternity temple and song are one. Within great cathedrals, built to acoustical perfection, the music echoes and resonates throughout. This leaves the impression that the stone itself is emitting the sound and the sound constitutes the stone.

Unlike Aslan's song, God's litany of Creation is inaudible. Nevertheless, God "plays" his song on Creation: let us think of Creation as his musical ensemble. The matins service of the Armenian Orthodox Church includes a week's cycle of hymns that celebrate God's acts of creation as recorded in Genesis. The Sunday hymn recalls the four primal elements — fire, earth, air, and water — that God has ordered into a harmony. The ancients believed that these four elements are opposites (or at least initially in contradiction to one another), such that, for example, air is hot and dry, whereas water is cold and wet. The hymn acknowledges this, while rejoicing, nonetheless, over the harmony that God has made from these seemingly antipodal elements:

> In the beginning the Word newly created
> the heaven of heavens out of nothing,
> and the celestial hosts
> of incorporeal intelligible watcher angels,
> and the sensible elements
> contrary one to another and yet agreeing,
> by which the ineffable Trinity
> is ever glorified.[5]

The ancients and the medievals called this harmony the "music of the spheres." Dante hears the music as he first enters heaven in the opening Canto of *The Paradisio*. "The song of God's glory," writes St. Gregory of Nyssa, is "produced by . . . a rhythm and composed of every creature with different qualities." The universe in all of its multifariousness is "an established order, . . . a well-arranged musical harmony" constituting an "ineffable hymn of God's power."[6]

"Beauty will save the world."

Fyodor Dostoyevsky, *The Idiot*

English translations of the book of Genesis render the Hebrew word *tob* as "good," as in, "And God saw that it was good." Nevertheless, the meaning of *tob* is broader than the

English "good." *Tob* also connotes "beautiful." Indeed, the Greek Septuagint version of the Old Testament — which is the text that the early church read and used liturgically — chooses not the Greek *agathos* ("good") to translate *tob*, but rather *kalos* ("beautiful").

Kalos may connote good in so much as what is beautiful, what is in conformity to God's thought and purpose, is good. *Kalos* normally refers to some "thing," or "object," like a statue, that is attractive to the eye. It is debated to what degree pictorial art played a role in ancient Israel's worship, but it is certainly safe to say that Israel excelled in vocal art and that both its material and vocal art reflected an appreciation of the beauty of Creation.

But not even *kalos* captures all the connotations of *tob*. For *tob* also connotes encounter, meeting, and response. God says, "Let there be," or "Let this happen." And when God "sees" what he has brought into existence, God joyfully *responds*. God breaks into song and proclaims, *"How good are the things that I have made! How appropriate! How fitting! How beautiful they are!"*

God is not an art critic who makes aesthetic judgments; nor is God a philosopher who issues metaphysical definitions or ethical decrees. God is more like a cantor who chants his Creation into existence and rejoices everlastingly over its beautiful harmony. His song continues, and its melody moves and inspires humankind to restore beauty and harmony to a Creation that is fallen and misshapen.

The Melody of Faith

I am the Alpha and the Omega, the Beginning and the End, the First and the Last.

Revelation 22:13, NKJV

The book of Genesis numbers six days over which God calls the whole Creation ensemble into existence, and on a seventh day, God rests. If one asks where or when to locate these days, Genesis answers, "In the beginning." Yet we cannot attribute duration to God, neither in terms of days that are consecutive nor otherwise. God is eternal, infinite, and immutable. Likewise, "Beginning" in the ordinary sense, as the start of a day or a year or a century, does not apply to God any more than "End," at least not in the temporal sense. Rather, "I am the Alpha and the Omega" is emblematic of eternity, or that which transcends temporality. Any attempt to correlate or conform this language of Genesis and Revelation with the human experience of time or with scientific cosmology is bound to founder on the shoals of a profound mystery which the ancient authors respected and did not try to explain.

"Day" and "evening," "beginning" and "end" are tropes, figures of speech, that the ancient Hebrew poet and the author of Revelation employed in order to account for both this wondrous Creation ensemble that God has brought into existence and the experience that all things temporal have a beginning and an end.

Since time commences when the world comes into existence, Genesis's "In the beginning" cannot refer to a tempo-

The Litany of Creation

ral moment but "marks," rather, the emergence of some *thing* new. In his theological discourse on the Work of Six Days, titled in Greek the *Hexaemeron,* St. Basil the Great of the fourth century explains, "The beginning of the road is not yet the road, and that of the house not yet the house; so the beginning of time is not yet time." Neither is it possible to divide the beginning in two or three, and so on, because this leads to an infinity of divisions. "It is ridiculous to imagine a beginning of a beginning," states Basil. Thus, when Scripture says, "In the beginning God created," this teaches us "that at the will of God the world arose in less than an instant."[7]

"Creation is *continual,*" writes Metropolitan Kallistos Ware. "If we are to be accurate when speaking of creation, we should not use the past tense but the continuous present.... Creation is not an event in the past, but a relationship in the present. If God did not continue to exert his creative will at every moment [from all eternity], the universe would immediately lapse into non-being."[8] In the words of St. Philaret, Metropolitan of Moscow in the nineteenth century: "All creatures are balanced upon the creative word of God, as if upon a bridge of diamond; above them is the abyss of the divine infinitude, below them that of their own nothingness."[9]

Yet even such words as *unceasing* and *continuous* can mislead when we apply them to God's act of Creation, since they are suggestive of duration — of past, present, and future time — which we cannot attribute to God any more than we can ascribe bodily or spatial dimension to God. "All things are immediate to God," says St. Gregory of Nazianzus of the fourth century. "Time for me is fractured in this way,/with some things earlier, others later; but for God it all comes in one,/and the great Godhead engulfs it in his arms."[10]

Likewise, the end of time, or the close of this *aeon,* is not a mere temporal event. No clock will mark it; no history book or scientific journal will record it. Where or when time ceases there simply is eternity. Time *will* end, but Creation *will not* cease to exist. God "created all things that they might have being" (Wis. 1:14, NEB). "The form of this [present] world is passing away" (1 Cor. 7:31, NKJV). But Creation will not vanish. It will, instead, come into another form, its own creaturely shape of eternity, in which there will be no counting of days and nights (Rev. 22:5). In his novel *The Sound and the Fury,* William Faulkner writes, "Clocks slay time. . . . Time is dead as long as it is being clicked off by little wheels; only when the clock stops does time come to life."[11]

"The word of the Lord endures forever" (1 Peter 1:25, NKJV). The image of Creation is eternally "before" God. It does not pass from his "sight." Likewise, his liturgy continues into the New Creation, a "new song" (Rev. 5:9-13, NKJV) of Life that men and angels sing together, glorifying God.

I think that Christians today spend far too much time and effort trying to prove and justify the truth of the Bible's and the church's teachings about Creation with respect to the most recent scientific theories on the origins, formation, and constitution of the universe. The search for such justifications and "proofs" may be intriguing, even at times edifying, but this does not draw us nearer to God or to that "peace of God, which surpasses all understanding" (Phil. 4:7, NKJV). For what does St. Paul say about this? "Be anxious for nothing, but in everything by prayer and supplication, with thanksgiving, let your requests be known to God" (Phil. 4:6, NKJV).

What is more, endeavors to present a doctrine of Creation or a theory of cosmology in synchrony with scientific theory risk the introduction of serious misconceptions about God and his relation to the Creation. Consider, for example, a belief many hold that God is the cause of Creation. But God is no more the cause of Creation than are the so-called laws of physics, chemistry, and biology. God does not "cause" Creation as striking a match ignites a flame. God does not "make" the world as a bird builds its nest. Nor do we salvage our notion of God as cause of everything by describing God as the First Cause or Prime Mover that initiates the great sequence of causes and effects that science calls Nature.

On occasion, theologians speak of God as "cause," with the qualification that "cause" is emptied of its ordinary connotations of temporality and spatiality or necessity and determinacy; but this is to say no more than that divine agency is analytically precedent (first in order) to Creation.[12] The eighteenth-century philosopher David Hume argued that what we call causality is merely our habituated expectation, based upon repeated experience, that certain events follow certain patterns and that these patterns will repeat themselves. Hume scandalized religious and nonreligious alike with his radical skepticism. Yet his observation is a useful place to start when speaking of God and God's relation to Creation. We cannot get behind the cosmic event in order to record or verify how it began. Scientists talk about a "Big Bang" by which the universe began. This intrigues some. "So this is the scientist's way of saying, 'In the beginning,'" some conclude. But no one has seen the Big Bang or heard it. And no one will. And none can prove or disprove that there was not some thing that was before it. The Big Bang is a hypothesis, also a metaphor, not a proof that Genesis is scientifically true.

We cannot know God in his eternity, nor should we attribute to God operations of nature. We should take care not to project our habitual expectations and ways of thinking onto God. "My thoughts are not your thoughts, neither are your ways my ways, says the LORD" (Isa. 55:8, RSV). Better to heed the counsel of St. Gregory of Nyssa: "Now as for the question of precisely how any single thing came into existence, we must banish it altogether from our discussion." All that need be said is "that the movement of God's Will becomes at any moment that He pleases a fact, and the intention becomes at once realized in Nature."[13]

The language of cause and effect entails the logic of necessity. For example, fire necessarily produces heat. Yet Creation does not issue from God in such a manner. Nothing compels God, who wants for naught, to bring something in addition to himself into existence. God freely chooses to bring the Creation into existence, while "how" he does so remains a mystery. More accurately, God loves Creation into existence perfectly freely, for perfect love is perfect freedom.

Where there are freedom and love there is personhood also. As God is love, so God is Person. The Father's love not only engenders the Son but also breathes forth the Holy Spirit, while the three are an eternal Communion of Being. The Triune God calls into existence beings other than itself.

The Litany of Creation

The Creation, the immense diversity of the universe, is God's ecstatic recapitulation of the plenitude of his Triune Being. The contemporary Orthodox theologian David Bentley Hart extends the analogy to musicality: "As God is Trinity, in whom all difference is possessed as perfect peace and unity, the divine life might be described as infinite music, and creation too might be described as music whose intervals, transitions, and phrases are embraced within God's eternal, Triune polyphony."[14] *Creation is a Trinitarian love song.* The Triune circle of God's love opens onto Creation, and God sustains it from "moment" to "moment" with his love.

But where and how in relation to God does Creation exist? Although theologians since at least St. Athanasius of the fourth century have spoken of Creation as "external" to God or outside of God, Athanasius himself would admit that externality and internality, like temporality and spatiality, are not attributable to God or our relationship to him.[15] They are, rather, modalities of creaturely existence. There is no "outside" or "inside" of God, who is infinite and eternal. The Creation is "other" than God, but not "external" to God, as the shed is to its builder. God's love calls into existence the "other" whose image God in his wisdom (Ps. 104:24) has entertained from eternity, and this very love bridges the gulf of being between divinity and the creature. Thus, it is possible to say that "God is in the world and the world is in God,"[16] remembering also that God transcends such categories as existence and nonexistence and in and out.

The love of God is not other than God, rather *who* God is in his personal identity as communion of Father, Son, and Holy Spirit. Through his love, God brings us into existence and sustains our being. His love dwells "within" us through the grace of the Holy Spirit, and draws us into communion with him (1 John 4:16) as if he were our very selves. Therefore, who or what God loves, other than himself, God "embraces" eternally. [17]

"The world is not opposed to eternity," states the Romanian theologian Dumitru Staniloae, "nor is the world in itself a linear eternity. It has its origin in eternity, is sustained by eternity, and is destined to become everlasting in a kind of eternity that is not identical with that of God. For the world is not eternal through itself, but through God."[18] God is ever-present to his Creation and is "within" it inasmuch as his love perpetually permeates it and draws it to him. Even as we mark time, even as we count the days and nights, even as we experience our life as a finite duration and time as a relentless series of stop-and-go, we live "within" eternity, and eternity is "inside of" us (Luke 17:21). Yet we are so distracted and disoriented by our anxieties, our thoughts, our fears, and our passions that we imagine that eternity and the kingdom of God, with its peace and harmony, is "elsewhere" or for "another day."

In his *Journals*, Father Alexander Schmemann ruminates, "It seems to me that eternity might be not the stopping of time, but precisely its resurrection and gathering. The fragmentation of time, its division, is the fall of eternity. Maybe the words of Christ are about time when He said: '. . . not to destroy anything but will raise it on the last day'" (John 6:39). "Eternal life," Schmemann suggests with great wisdom, may not be "what begins after temporal life," but rather "the eternal presence of the totality of life."[19]

The Litany of Creation

The human presence within the world transforms the world into a realm of liturgy. The divinely created beauty of the world moves man to praise God and the world becomes the space in which man's offering of praise [to God] is celebrated.

Hieromonk Gregorios,
"Cosmos as a Realm of Liturgy"

St. Gregory of Nyssa describes the Creation as a hymn of glory to God. It is, he says, a kind of "musical harmony," a blend of "various separate elements" with a "constant rhythm" ordering "all the parts" into "a supremely consonant melody."[20] In the ninth century, St. Nicephorus of Constantinople describes the Trisagion hymn "Holy, Holy, Holy" (from Isaiah in his vision of the temple at Jerusalem [Isa. 6:3]) and the whole liturgical ensemble of icons, priestly ministrations, songs, and prayers as "a melody of theology"[21] expressive of the ineffable mystery of the divine will.

It is our human vocation to translate or transcribe God's intelligible, eternal, transcendent liturgy into sensible speech and action. Doing God's will is not merely morality. More important, it is joining in song to sing God's hymn of Creation so that all things may be made perfect. Short of this participation in God's Trinitarian love song, we cannot hope to comprehend the deep, deep meaning of Creation and our common destiny with it.

In a fallen world, however, sin and death preface liturgy: what should be an unhindered path to holy knowledge, harmony, and joy is marred by ignorance, discord, and suffering. The constant cacophony of a fallen Creation interrupts the melody of faith and drowns it out almost everywhere. Worship is sacrificial until Christ, the New or Second Adam, renders up his sinless and holy life on the Cross as the final bloody sacrifice. "Christ came as High Priest of the good things to come, with the greater and more perfect tabernacle not made with hands, that is, not of this creation" (Heb. 9:11, NKJV). In Christ, in his perfected humanity, the church, the temple of Creation, is rebuilt and the song is renewed.

Vladimir Lossky observes that the saint whose will is in perfect accord with God's will "perceives the world as a 'musical arrangement': in each thing he hears a word of the Word."[22] Alexander Schmemann extends this thought to the church gathered in liturgy. He argues that the melismatic hymnody of the ancient church with the singing of the alleluia is a greeting "in the most profound sense":[23] the appearance of God in Jesus Christ. It is the beginning of a melody that the church alone sings until the song is complete at the New Creation.

The Bible tells us that the universe is *anthropocentric* for a *theocentric* purpose: the glorification of God in and through all of Creation. Man is the microcosm. Within the human being, spiritual and sensible worlds meet. Man, whom God has created in his own image as a personal and free being, contains within himself all of the categories of existence and, therefore, is uniquely able to draw all of Creation into the "circle" of God's Triune fellowship. The liturgy of the Christian Eucharist recapitulates God's creative, redemptive, and sanctifying work in Christ, whilst also

The Litany of Creation

through the symbols of the bread and wine it brings the whole world before God, sanctified by the Spirit and transformed into an unspoiled New Creation.

Christians make sense of Creation doxologically and liturgically. Christian liturgy and worship unfold and illumine spiritual knowledge and wisdom about Creation that modern life forgets.

. . . and the Spirit of God hovered over the surface of the water.
Genesis 1:2, REB

[Jesus] was baptized in the Jordan by John. As he was coming up out of the water, he saw the heavens break open and the Spirit descend upon him, like a dove.
Mark 1:9-10, REB

He [Christ] was with God at the beginning, and through him all things came to be.
John 1:2-3, REB

Water, the most plastic of all substances, is a symbol in Genesis of Creation itself, of the vast potentiality of a still, formless world waiting to be made a universe, a cosmos of order and harmony. Water is the deepest symbol of life itself, for without water there is no life. Thus, it should not be surprising that of all the feasts of the church, Epiphany — the celebration in Orthodox Christianity of the baptism of Jesus in the waters of the Jordan River — is a pre-eminent expression of the liturgy of Creation. Epiphany reveals that the one whom John the Forerunner baptizes in the Jordan River is the Creator-Word through whom God brings all things into existence and binds the universe together. At Epiphany the Spirit descends upon Jesus like a dove (Mark 1:10): this is the same Creator-Spirit who hovered over the primal waters in the beginning.

Epiphany celebrates Creation and its renewal in Christ. The Great Compline of the Byzantine service announces, "Christ is baptized. He carries up the world."[24] Only he who is the Creator-Word, Lord of Heaven and Earth, can carry the world, cleansed, refreshed, and renewed, up out of the waters and offer it back to God. During the Matins service, worshippers celebrate in joyful song this day of the New Creation:

> The creation finds itself set free,
> And those in darkness are now made sons of light. . . .
> Let the whole earthly creation clothe itself in white,
> For this day it is raised up from its fall from heaven.
> The Word who preserves all things
> Has cleansed it in the flowing waters:
> Washed and resplendent, it has escaped from its
>   former sins.[25]

"Once again, a beginning," writes Alexander Schmemann in a homily on Epiphany. "Once again, we experi-

The Litany of Creation

ence the world joyfully and we see its beauty and harmony as God's gift. Once again, we give thanks. And in this thanksgiving, praise, and joy, we once again become genuine human beings."[26]

All of the Eastern churches celebrate Epiphany with a great hymn of the blessing of the waters. The church recalls the biblical stories of Creation, Fall, and Exile; and it rejoices over the birth in the Jordan River of the New Creation. The Armenian hymn of the Blessing of the Waters recollects God's act of bringing "being out of not-being," as he compacted the earth from the primal "four elements." "Today," continues the hymn, "earth's face is renewed at the appearing of God. . . . Today the shut and barred gate of the garden is opened to mankind."[27] The Byzantine hymn of water blessing announces, "Today we have purchased the Kingdom of Heaven; for the Lord's Kingdom shall have no end./ Today earth and sea share the joy of the world, and the world is filled with gladness."[28]

These hymns for Epiphany remind us that Creation and Redemption are really two sides of a single coin. The Creator-Word *is* the Redeemer-Word. There is never a "time" when God stops creating in order to redeem or stops redeeming in order to re-create. The same waters that existed at the beginning of the Old Creation are present at the beginning of the New Creation, only they must now be exorcized of the demonic presence. It is not that Christ's body is cleansed in the Jordan, but, rather, it is that Christ purifies the waters and prepares them for the Holy Spirit, who sweeps over them to engender new life within them as it did in the beginning. The hymn of the Armenian Church proclaims, "And having washed all clean from the stain of sin, arraying them in fresh plumage, and having sealed them with the impress of the cross for one flock and one shepherd, . . . [the Son] elected them into his fold, the catholic church. . . . Today the grace of the Holy Spirit, hallowing the water, becomes co-worker [with Christ]. . . . Today come the currents of grace of the Holy Spirit and creatures are inundated [refreshed] therewith." [29]

Wherefore we also celebrate with gladness the eighth day in which Jesus also rose from the dead, and was made manifest, and ascended into Heaven.

Epistle of Barnabas, 15:8

After eight days, may the octave-day be for you a great feast.

Apostolic Constitutions, 5:19

The *Epistle of Barnabas* comes to us from either the late first or early second century. It testifies to the ancient theology of the "eighth day," the belief that the Hebrew Sunday is not only the first day of the Old Creation but also that the Resurrection of Jesus Christ reveals it as the eighth day on which a New Creation begins. The *Apostolic Constitutions* of fourth-century origins speak to the extension of this concept of the "octave" to feasts other than Easter.

The Litany of Creation

This theology of the eighth day, or octave, is then rooted in the Easter event. Every Sunday, henceforth, belongs to and also breaks from the weekly cycle of ordinary time into a new *aeon*, a New Creation, so that Christians live from Sunday to Sunday. Each week the church lives "into" the New Creation through the liturgy. There is a profound difference between the modern habit of living from weekend to weekend and the Christian rhythm of the week. The *re-creation* of the first and eighth day is radically different from the recreation of a secular weekend.[30] The *Apostolic Constitutions* specifically prescribe that the eighth day after certain major feasts be called the octave. Strictly speaking, the octave repeats the feast's celebration, and normally this falls on the Sunday following the feast. The octave is not just a repetition of the feast, however. It deepens important dimensions of that feast, or makes more explicit that feast's connection with other important Christian beliefs and practices. Epiphany, Easter, and Pentecost are exemplary of the octave in early Christian worship.

Easter, however, is the paradigm of the octave in which the church affirms its belief in the intimate and inseparable connection between Creation, Redemption, and New Creation. St. Gregory of Nazianzus explains the importance of the Easter octave, or the first Sunday and eighth day after Easter. He writes that whereas Easter is pre-eminently the "anniversary of our salvation, this [first Sunday after Easter] is ... of the second creation, so that as the first creation began on Sunday ... , so the second creation began [also] on a Sunday."[31]

The Armenian Church still follows the ancient Christian

tradition closely. Whereas in many churches Eastern and Western, the first Sunday following Easter is given the name Thomas Sunday,[32] the Armenian Church continues to call it New Sunday (or Second Easter). Not surprisingly, the central theme of New Sunday is the New Creation. In the Armenian service, the first seventeen verses of the Gospel of John are chief among the lectionary readings. They, of course, echo the Creation narrative of Genesis. John speaks of Christ as the Divine Word "who was with God . . . in the beginning" (John 1:1-2, NKJV) and through whom God has made all things (John 1:3). Again echoing the first chapter of Genesis, John 1:18–2:11 records seven days, the first week of the New Creation.[33] On the seventh day, Jesus performs the first of seven great signs that reveals the New Creation is commenced. He symbolically turns old, stale water into the best wine at a wedding in Cana of Galilee (John 2:1-11). "The jars [at the wedding feast] destined for the 'ablutions among the Jews' are hardly sufficient, but 'ancient forms [that] have passed away,'" writes Paul Evdokimov.[34] A new age *(aeon)* has begun, of which the water transformed to wine is a baptismal image. The wedding itself is a sign and emblem of the marriage of the Lamb and the church that the book of Revelation (19:7-8) celebrates.

The Great Canon of the Armenian liturgy for New Sunday proclaims, "Today, the awful sound of Gabriel's trumpet rang out/Announcing the good news to the universe./The angels in never-ceasing voice sang a new hymn. . . ./Let us sing a new song in a voice never silent."[35] Though they refer to the empty tomb and the Resurrection, these verses also allude to the scene in the Heavenly Temple of the book of

The Litany of Creation

Revelation wherein there is sung "a new song" (Rev. 5:9, NKJV). The hymn calls Christ "the New Tabernacle," and the church is Christ's body. This "new song" sung in the New Tabernacle is an everlasting song. It is the perfection of all the songs and hymns that Israel and the church have sung thanking and praising God. Three doxological melodies comprise this "new song" (Rev. 5:9b-10, 12, 13b), all of which are dedicated to Christ, the Lamb, who sits on the throne and inaugurates the new age, and a new heaven and a new earth (Rev. 21:1).

In the early church, those newly baptized on Easter removed their white robes on the octave and then returned to their normal lives. They were no longer the old humanity under servitude to sin and condemned to death, however. Now they were the new humanity alive in the Spirit, proud inheritors of the kingdom of heaven. The Armenian Canon reflects this ancient practice:

> Today, you, sons of Sion,
> By grace born sons of God in the font
> In order that the temple of human nature be renewed,
> Praise the Bridegroom who emerged
> From the bridal chamber of the new tomb,
> Declaring, May your resurrection be glorified![36]

The hymn describes a church adorned with a fresh and resplendent "garment woven from gold," and also a "crown." In her, living waters renew and replenish the earth. A communion prayer of the Armenian liturgy calls the holy apostles "the cleansers of the whole world."[37] The church herself is the cosmos restored to its former beauty, as "all the universe has been adorned in a new garment,"[38] bedecked for the great marriage of the Lamb (Rev. 19:7).

The liturgy of Creation, like the rivers of Paradise and the New Jerusalem, runs through the whole of the Christian life and this passing age. This liturgy is no mere doctrine, nor theory about the origins of the universe and life. It is, rather, the church in movement from the old *aeon* into the new. The enduring love and sacrifice of the Word who became flesh and the restorative and sanctifying power of the Holy Spirit make possible this passage.

CHAPTER 2

The Luminous Moment of the Apocalypse

Soul: When do you come, my salvation?
Jesus: I come, your portion.
Soul: I wait with oil burning.
Jesus: Throw open the hall.
Soul: I open the hall
Both: for the heavenly feast,
Soul: come, Jesus!
Jesus: come, dear soul!

Johann Sebastian Bach, Cantata 140

We have explored the meaning that Creation holds for Christians. We saw that the church joins its voice to the liturgy through which God calls the world into being and sustains it. Christians grasp the meaning of Creation through their worship of its maker. Whatever knowledge they may gain of Creation from formal theological or philosophical discourse, or a "doctrine" of Creation, it is second to the understanding apprehended through their thanksgiving to God for all that he has made.

The Melody of Faith

In the strict sense, Chapter 1 was about the "beginning." Yet, as we saw, Christian reflection on the "beginning" necessarily brings into view the "end." When we consider the Apocalypse, we must keep in mind God's act of Creation; for just as talk of the beginning necessitates talk of the end, so also to properly view the Apocalypse, we must consider Creation. Indeed, the Christian life is a process of living in the paradox and mystery of beginning and end. "Apocalypse" derives from the Greek *apocalypsis,* which means "to unveil" or "to expose to full view." The Apocalypse is that luminous "moment" at the margin of time and eternity when Christ returns in glory to judge the living and the dead, and establishes "the new heavens and a new earth" (2 Pet. 3:13, NKJV). It is that "moment" through which the whole course of Creation and its meaning are completely clarified.

Efforts to comprehend the nature of the Apocalypse that give little or no thought to the liturgical life of the Church are misguided. Today a vast "science" of exegesis and scriptural interpretation has arisen in the endeavor to read history "into" or "out from" the symbolic speech of the Bible in order to predict the "moment" of the end. The truth of God's scriptural revelation about the last things is best understood through the church's liturgical actions; for, as we shall see, the Apocalypse is a liturgical prolepsis, an event that anticipates its own future fulfillment. It is to the liturgy we must turn for an understanding of the Apocalypse, but first we will contemplate the paradoxical presence of Christ.

The Luminous Moment of the Apocalypse

"Today you will be with Me in Paradise."

Luke 23:43, NKJV

Science and history also fail us when it comes to understanding the paradox of our Savior's presence. Christians pray, as the Only-Begotten Son has instructed them: "Thy Kingdom come. Thy will be done in earth, as it is in heaven" (Matt. 6:10, KJV). Christ hears their supplication and draws near in his Spirit; his kingdom grows within and among the people of faith whom the Spirit visits. For Christ has promised: "Where two or three are gathered together in My name, I am there in the midst of them" (Matt. 18:20, NKJV); "Lo, I am with you always, even to the end of the age" (Matt. 28:20, NKJV). Yet, how is this possible when, forty days after his resurrection, Jesus ascended to the Father in Heaven so that the angels declared, "This same Jesus, who was taken up from you into heaven, will so come in like manner as you see Him go into heaven" (Acts 1:11, NKJV)? If Jesus is with us, "even to the end of the age," how is it that for two millennia, Christians have joined their voices with St. John, who at the close of his Revelation, beseeches: "Come, Lord Jesus!" (Rev. 22:20, NKJV)?

This is the paradox: Christ is near, yet he is afar. On Holy Friday, Jesus calls from the Cross to the penitent thief, "Today you will be with Me in Paradise" (Luke 23:43, NKJV). Yet on this same day, Jesus' friends lovingly place his shattered body in a newly hewn tomb. On Holy Saturday, while his body still lies in the grave, Christ's spirit descends to the prison of Hades and frees the dead who, since Adam and Eve, have disobeyed God (1 Pet. 3:19-20). Furthermore, Christ is present in the Eucharist, but he continues to be at the right hand of his Father in Heaven.

In spite of all this, the New Testament would have us expect Christ to return in glory at the end of this age. It calls this "Second Coming" of Christ the Parousia. In the thirteenth chapter of St. Mark's Gospel, often referred to as the "small apocalypse," Jesus echoes the words of the prophet Daniel (Dan. 7:13) when he explains to Peter, James, John, and Andrew that the day will arrive when the people "see the Son of Man coming in the clouds with great power and glory" (Mark 13:26, NKJV). In the Gospel of St. Matthew, Jesus announces the Parousia and relates several parables that emphasize the need for his followers to be watchful for this event (Matt. 24:29ff.). Likewise, St. Paul compares the "coming of the Lord" to that of "a thief in the night" (1 Thess. 5:2, NKJV).

Metropolitan John Zizioulas helps us understand when he writes: "The truth [which is the Word of God] is located simultaneously at the heart of history, at the ground of creation, and at the end of history."[1] God is the eternal "I am," (Exod. 3:14, RSV), the Existing One. Should it be any surprise that the Greek root of *parousia* means "to be present"? All of the discrete temporal events in Jesus' life — his birth, baptism, transfiguration, crucifixion, resurrection, and ascension — are manifestations of the one Divine Presence that transcends time and chronology. This we must keep in mind as we explore what the Liturgy tells us about the Apocalypse.

The Luminous Moment of the Apocalypse

"Blessed is he that cometh in the name of the Lord."

Matthew 21:9, KJV

The church confesses its belief in two comings of Jesus Christ, who is, after all, the "Alpha and the Omega, the Beginning and the End, the First and the Last" (Rev. 22:13, NKJV). Jesus first came in humility and weakness as a helpless child, but will come a second time at the end of this age in power and glory. St. Cyril of Jerusalem of the fourth century expounds: "The first [coming] was unobserved, *like rain on a fleece* (Ps. 72.6)";[2] the second will be "open. . . . In his former advent, he [Christ] was wrapped in swaddling clothes in a manger; in his second coming, *He covereth Himself with light as with a garment* (Ps. 104.2)." In his first coming, Christ "*endureth the Cross, despising shame* (Heb. 12.2); in His second, He comes attended by a host of Angels."[3] Orthodox icons of the Nativity indicate these two comings when they depict the infant Jesus wrapped in glistening white swaddling clothes, clothes that foreshadow both his death and burial and his Second Coming in a garment of pure light.

St. Cyril commends the use in the liturgy of the appellation "Blessed is he who comes," known as the *Benedictus qui venit*, to indicate both of Christ's comings: "At this first coming we said, *Blessed is He that cometh in the name of the Lord* (Matt. 21:9, 23:39), so we will repeat the same at this second coming."[4] Christian theologians and scholars speculate that the *Benedictus qui venit* was preceded in early Christian prayer and worship by the Aramaic phrase *Maranatha,* which is commonly translated as "Come, Lord Jesus," but which can also mean "Our Lord has come."[5] There is evidence that the very earliest Christians used the phrase as a prayer of greeting or declaration of faith, in one or quite possibly both of these meanings.

The substitution of the *Benedictus qui venit* for *Maranatha* in Christian liturgy may explain why St. Cyril emphasizes that the *Benedictus qui venit* should be used in reference to *both* of Christ's "comings." This is certainly how the phrase functions in the ancient Liturgy of the Armenian Church. It is chanted after the Great Entrance, the solemn procession in which the bread and wine are brought to the altar. It is a hinge that joins the Great Entrance with the offertory and the Kiss of Peace. This portion of the liturgy is a powerfully anamnestic expression of the ancient church's eschatological expectation; for here the Apocalypse is proleptically enfolded within the church's remembrance of Christ's life, passion, and resurrection on earth.

At the start of the Eucharistic offertory, precedent to the Cherubic Hymn,[6] a responsory comprised of verses from several psalms and a passage from Habakkuk celebrates the great eschatological wedding of the Lamb of God with his bride the church. Christ, who was resurrected at the rising of the sun, will likewise return in the East mounted on the sun. Mount Paran in the book of Habakkuk represents Mount Sinai, the place of holy theophany. At the end of this age, God in Christ reveals himself once again, but this time in the fullness of his glory:

The Luminous Moment of the Apocalypse

The Deacon
> In the sun has he set his tabernacle; and he comes forth as a bridegroom out of his chamber.
> Ps. 19(18):4, LXX

The Clerks (or Choir)
> And he rejoices as a giant to run his course.
> Ps. 19(18):5, LXX

The Deacon
> Cast up a highway for him who rides upon the heaven of heavens toward the east.
> Ps. 68(67):33, LXX
> God shall come from the south; and the holy One from Mount Paran.   Hab. 3:3, LXX[7]

The Prayer of the Great Entrance that follows includes a second companionate responsory comprised of Psalm 24(23):7-10. It is both a prophecy of Jesus' triumphal entry into Jerusalem on Palm Sunday and his Second Coming. The Deacon twice calls: "Lift up the gates, O princes; let the everlasting doors be lifted up, and the king of glory shall come in." The priest first responds, "Who is the king of glory? The Lord strong in his power, the Lord mighty in battle." The priest then asks, "Who is the king of glory? — The Lord of hosts," and the deacon affirms, "Even he is the king of glory!"[8]

At this point, the celebrant lays the gifts on the altar table and proclaims: "Let us stand in prayer before the holy altar of God that we may find the grace of mercy in the day of appearing at the second coming of our Lord and Savior Jesus Christ."[9] Here the full meaning of everything that has transpired coalesces: the Eucharistic liturgy is itself a prolepsis of the glorious return of Christ, the luminous moment of the Apocalypse, the advent of the kingdom of God. Alexander Schmemann comments: "The messianic Kingdom or life in the new aeon is 'actualized' — becomes real — in the assembly of the Church, in the *ekklesia* when the believers come together to have communion in the Lord's body."[10]

After the celebrant has placed the host upon the altar, the congregation joyfully exchanges the Kiss of Peace. They not only physically embrace one another as a sign of love and unity, but they also affirm in their greetings this liturgical experience of the Parousia: "Christ is revealed in our midst," is followed by "Blessed is the revelation of Christ." As this exchange is made throughout the church, the choir sings the hymn:

> Christ in our midst has been revealed;
> He Who is God, is here seated.
> The voice of peace has resounded;
> Holy greeting is commanded.
> This Church has now become one soul;
> The kiss is given for a full bond;
> The enmity has been removed;
> And love is spread over us all.[11]

Schmemann explains that at this moment in Orthodox liturgies, the assembly enters "the Eschaton [the end of the Old and the beginning of the New Creation], and [stands]

The Luminous Moment of the Apocalypse

beyond time and space. It is because all this has first happened," he continues, "that something will happen to bread and wine."[12] Yes, the Eucharist is a commemorative meal, but it also is a meeting in which the Lord Jesus Christ manifests himself to the church in his complete glory, "the same [Presence] yesterday, today, and forever" (Heb. 13:8, NKJV). Partakers of this meal, participants in this liturgy, are now and not yet, "caught up in the clouds to meet the Lord in the air" (1 Thess. 4:14, NKJV) at his Second Coming.

Veni Creator Spiritus *(Come, Holy Spirit)*

Thus it is that the Apocalypse unfolds within the Eucharist. As the members of the assembly consume the body and the blood of Christ, the Word assimilates them into himself. They become his Body, his Holy Presence. But none of this is possible without the third Person of the Trinity, the Holy Spirit. It is the power of the Holy Spirit that transforms the people into Christ's Body and enables them to experience Christ's presence. It is in and through the Holy Spirit that Christ is present from Pentecost until the end of this age.

The Anaphora (the prayers of offering) in the Armenian Liturgy includes the Eucharistic Prayer of remembrance and the words of institution that state explicitly that the bread and wine are the body and blood of Christ. Although the Holy Spirit is present throughout the liturgy, the Spirit is particularly invoked at this moment to reveal that Christ is present in the bread and wine, to manifest them as his life-giving body and blood. The celebrant prays: "We bow down and beseech and ask thee, beneficent God, send upon us and upon these gifts set forth, thy coeternal and consubstantial Spirit."[13] This translation of the bread and wine into the body and blood of Christ fulfills proleptically what began with the descent of the Holy Spirit upon the apostles at Pentecost. Paul Evdokimov explains, "The fulfillment of history is beyond the limits of the Church *in situ,* which, living in the light of the second coming of Christ, is actually in history, realizing and accomplishing it."[14]

Pentecost is the foundation for the understanding of the Eucharistic assembly as not just a sign of the Parousia, but as the Parousia's proleptic fulfillment. On Pentecost the church comes to know itself as the eschatological kernel of the heavenly kingdom. This is the significance of Peter's pronouncement to those assembled on Pentecost that "what was spoken to the prophet Joel" has been fulfilled. "'And it shall come to pass in the last days, says God, that I will pour out of My Spirit on all flesh'" (Acts 2:16-17, NKJV). Zizioulas writes that on Pentecost "through the outpouring of the Holy Spirit, the 'last days' enter into history, while the unity of humanity [in the Body of Christ] is affirmed."[15]

During the Communion, the congregation reaffirms what was said at the Kiss of Peace. They proclaim: "Our God and our Lord has appeared to us." And they repeat the *Benedictus qui venit:* "Blessed is he who comes in the name of the Lord."[16] Yet, this appearance, this coming, of Christ in the Eucharist is not, as sometimes interpreted, the "repetition" of his advent. It is, rather, the lifting up of the Church

The Luminous Moment of the Apocalypse

into the Parousia. It is "the Church's participation in his [Christ's] heavenly glory,"[17] the glory of the cosmic Pentecost when Christ returns, accompanied by the fire of the Holy Spirit that does not destroy this world, but instead transfigures and renews it.

> "Yes," said Aslan, though they had not spoken. "While he lay dreaming his name was Time. Now that he is awake he will have a new one."
>
> C. S. Lewis, *The Last Battle*

C. S. Lewis might have had in mind a different meaning for these words that the Great Lion, Aslan, speaks as the world of Narnia comes to an end and the new Narnia is unveiled. Whatever Lewis's exact meaning or intention, Aslan's speech is suggestive of the paradox of time and the Parousia that we have been pondering. The Parousia is vastly different from the ordinary events of time and history, for it traverses and transcends before and after, yesterday and tomorrow, time and duration, chronology and history. As we saw in the preceding chapter, the Resurrection of Jesus Christ has transformed the first day of the week into an eighth day, or the first day of a New Creation. The eighth day is the "day of the Lord" that lies beyond the limits of the cycle of the ordinary week. It has no tomorrow after it or yesterday before it. It closes history but does not belong to it. Allow me to repeat St. Basil of Caesarea's description of this mystery:

The Lord's Day is great and glorious. The Scripture knows this day without evening, having no other day, a day without end; the psalmist called it the eighth day, since it is outside of time measured in weeks. Whether you call it a day or an age, it is all the same. If you call it an aeon, it is one, and not a part of a whole.[18]

If one follows Basil's logic, any attempt to predict when the Parousia will happen must be futile. This is because such a prediction assumes that it will be an ordinary day, that it might happen tomorrow or the next day or a hundred years from today. Jesus, in the Gospel of St. Mark, admonishes, "But of that day and hour no one knows, not even the angels in heaven, nor the Son, but only the Father" (Mark 13:32, NKJV). And St. Paul reiterates in his First Epistle to the church in Thessalonica, "But concerning the times and the seasons, brethren, you have no need that I should write to you. For you yourselves know perfectly that the day of the Lord so comes as a thief in the night" (1 Thess. 5:1-2, NKJV).

Sergius Bulgakov speaks eloquently of this when he writes: "[The Parousia] and the universal catastrophe [both] . . . will take place within the world's limits but [also] at its very boundary and in this sense *outside* its time. . . . The net of time is torn, and supertime suddenly shines through it — not as a calendar event but as something that transcends our time."[19] At the Parousia, time indeed, as Aslan says, will have a new name.

The Luminous Moment of the Apocalypse

The heavens will pass away with a great noise, and the elements will melt with fervent heat; both the earth and the works that are in it will be burned up.

2 Peter 3:10, NKJV

In those days, . . . they will see the Son of Man coming in the clouds with great power and glory.

Mark 13:24, 26, NKJV

In the Orthodox tradition there is no icon of the resurrection event itself. While the event claims historicity by virtue of those who witnessed Christ's post-resurrection appearances, it also transcends history and time. Thus, the Gospels do not describe the Resurrection in detail. However, there are icons that depict the events surrounding the Resurrection that the Bible does describe. The Orthodox tradition has settled on not one but two Easter icons. One is the Myrrh-Bearing Women at the Empty Tomb (included in every Gospel: Matthew 28, Mark 16, Luke 24, and John 20). The other is Christ's Harrowing of Hades, also called the Anastasis (Greek for "resurrection"), mentioned in Acts 2:14-28 and 1 Peter 3:18-19.

I wish to speak here for a moment of the Anastasis icon in particular. (See Plate 1.) Peter reports that following his death on the Cross, Jesus descended into Hades, Sheol in the Old Testament, to preach salvation to the dead. In Anastasis icons, Christ typically is the central figure. He is surrounded with a bright mandorla, adorned with a radiant halo, and clad in luminous golden-yellow or white garments and stands over the double crossed doors to the dark underworld, trampling them down with his feet. Beneath these doors in pitch-black darkness is a downcast Satan, or sometimes several demons desperately trying to escape. Broken chains, keys, and nails are scattered about, showing that Christ has destroyed the gates to Hades and overcome death. Christ may hold a scroll, which represents his preaching of the Resurrection to the dead, or sometimes his Cross as a symbol of victory. With one hand he lifts Adam out of Hades, and, with the other, Eve. Often righteous figures of the Old Testament and the New Testament are standing behind Adam and Eve, awaiting their liberation as well.

The descent into Hades is a super-temporal and super-spatial event, similar to the Resurrection, though not happening on terra firma itself. Nevertheless, the church assigns it a "time," which is Holy Saturday. This is because on Holy Friday Christ is crucified and is buried, and on Easter Sunday Christ is resurrected. Yet to the dead whom Christ visits, it is neither Saturday, nor any day of a week. The spatial references of the descent into Hades are symbolic; Hades is not a physical place, located north or south, east or west, up or down. The iconographic representation of Christ's body in Hades is symbolic also, consistent with the church's understanding that Christ's earthly body still lies in the tomb. The Harrowing of Hades is biblical mythos painted on wood.

That which is iconic and symbolic can be represented with painted images *or* with words. Images sometimes communi-

The Luminous Moment of the Apocalypse

cate truth and meaning that definition and explanation cannot. This is especially true regarding spiritual mysteries and transcendent realities that elude conceptualization. And in the case of 2 Peter and the Gospel of Mark, words act iconically and symbolically. They, like the imagery of the Anastasis icon, are mythic in character and indicate a reality that is transhistorical and super-temporal.

Yet today, as in the past, some seek to interpret these texts as if they are headlines from a newspaper that describe events which will happen some place in the world at an assigned time within history. Some seize upon the passages in 2 Peter and Mark 13 (and others like them in Scripture) to speculate about a frightening, violent, catastrophic end to the world. But, as I have suggested, these sorts of passages are not amenable to flat-footed interpretation as if they are mere history or science. They are better understood in and through the experience of the Eucharistic liturgy.

Just as bread and wine are not destroyed in the Eucharist in order to become body and blood, so also the Apocalypse does not bring the complete destruction of this world but instead transfigures it into the New Creation. The second-century Saint Irenaeus of Lyons is helpful in grasping the distinction between extermination and transformation. He rejects the notion that God will completely destroy his Creation: "Neither the substance nor the matter of the creation will be annihilated — true and solid is the one who established it." Rather, "everything is renewed. . . . For the one . . . who sits on the throne [has] said, 'Behold, I make all things new. . . . Write everything, for these words are faithful and true'" (Rev. 21:5).[20] By locating the truth in symbolic speech,

Irenaeus understands the reality that transcends history and science: the whole of Creation is renovated in Christ.

St. Paul says that "the fashion of this world passeth away" (1 Cor. 7:31, KJV). Sin, corruption, and death, which are its present form, must be removed so that the Lord might come again and the "old" might give way to the "new." There is not a total, radical discontinuity between the Old Creation and the New Creation as is implied by the kinds of interpretation that I mention above. "Something disappears, [yet] something remains," writes Paul Evdokimov. "It is not a simple separation of the things of this world, but a metamorphosis of chosen elements and their passage to the 'new earth' and 'new heaven.'"[21]

The Liturgy invites us to read the Bible typologically, which leads us to see that the cloud on which Jesus descends at the Parousia is the same as the pillar of cloud in Exodus. This cloud is the symbol of God's glory, a manifestation of the Holy Spirit, which makes the face of Moses shine on his descent from Sinai and causes Christ's garments to glisten on Mount Tabor. The fire that melts the earth in its elements is the same that lights the burning bush and issues from Elijah's heaven-bound chariot. It is also present in the flaming tongues that come to rest on the disciples at Pentecost. To believe that the "cloud" is material and the "fire" is heat is as much a mistake as imagining that "the day of the Lord" is just an ordinary day in the course of linear time and human history.

St. Peter's vision of the Apocalypse is typological and clearly concerns spiritual purification and renewal. He trains his eyes on "the new heavens and a new earth in which righteousness dwells" (2 Pet. 3:13, NKJV), wherein the Son is eternally present in the fullness of his glory. Peter looks forward to that day when our sinful humanity and this corrupted world will be hallowed, so that we, and it, are prepared as a proper dwelling place for the Holy One. Thus, he exhorts his reader to pay mind to "what manner of persons ought you to be in holy conduct and godliness" (2 Pet. 3:11, NKJV). He does not linger on descriptions of a world in cinders, of the elements dissolved, or of the whole universe sunken into a black hole; he does not intend that we think of literal fire and destruction. His aim is to inspire, not to terrorize.

The prophet Daniel tells the story of the trial in the fiery furnace of the three youths Shadrach, Meshach, and Abednego. While the soldiers who cast them into the fire were consumed by it, the youths were not (Dan. 3:19-28). Instead, as they sang hymns praising God, they were protected, as it were, by a "fourth" with them in the fire "like the Son of God" (Dan. 3:25, NKJV). Likewise, in the cosmic Pentecost of the Apocalypse everything that belongs to the kingdom of God will be protected and transfigured, while the remainder is consumed. The church, having been fashioned anew by the blood of Christ, takes up its "new song" of praise to the Lamb (Rev. 5:9, 14:3), and is joined by the whole Creation, in its *telos* of New Creation, at this luminous moment of the Apocalypse.

CHAPTER 3

Divine Therapy

Jesus then means according to the Hebrew "Savior," but in the Greek tongue "The Healer;" since he is physician of souls and bodies, curer of spirits, curing the blind in body, and leading minds into light.

St. Cyril of Jerusalem,
Catechetical Lectures, 10

Long before St. Cyril of Jerusalem took up the vision of divine therapy in the fourth century, it was already firmly established in the Christian imagination. Jesus' healing miracles, the story of the good Samaritan, and, of course, the Resurrection itself played no small part in making this so. Could there be any doubt, based upon the testimony of the Gospels, that Jesus Christ is the physician of our souls and bodies, and that salvation through him cures our mortal sickness and restores us to wholeness and health? In his *Catechetical Lectures,* St. Cyril turned to this venerable theme in order to prepare candidates for baptism and admission into the Eucharistic life of the church. In all likelihood, he did so not only because he believed that the theme of divine healing illumines the deepest truths about salvation, but also because he recognized that it is existentially compelling.

Over the centuries, Christian theologians and apologists have, of course, employed other biblical images effectively to speak about salvation. The bucolic metaphor of the good shepherd who gathers and guards his flock (Matt. 18:12-14; Luke 15:4-7; John 10:1-18), the military metaphor of spiritual combat led by Christ the victorious warrior (Matt. 12:29; Luke 11:21-22; Eph. 6:11-12), the metaphors of Christ the deliverer taken from juridical relations (Rom. 3:24-26; Heb. 9:15) and the ransom from sin and death (1 Tim. 2:6; Gal. 3:13) are among the most noteworthy of these images.[1]

St. Ephrem the Syrian, who, like St. Cyril, wrote in the fourth century, insists that the Divine Word "wore" these images and metaphors as garments of his incarnation. "He [Christ] clothed Himself in language," writes St. Ephrem, "so that He might clothe us in His mode of life." These images of shepherd, warrior, deliverer, physician, and the like do not, however, "apply to His true Being:/because that Being is hidden."[2] They are not literally attributable to his eternal identity. They are not his divine name.[3] Nonetheless, through these images, God has depicted how he effects salvation for us. They are God's temporal modes of self-revelation by which God has rendered himself comprehensible to us in some manner and made the divine grace visible to us. God has worn these images as sacramental signs of salvation that point to its source in the Divine Word.

St. Ephrem understood that none of these metaphors and

images can stand alone or completely illumine the meaning of salvation. Yet, at a particular moment in civilization, one may enjoy special power to reach and touch human hearts and minds. The therapeutic vision and its trinity of physician, treatment, and cure have this power today due to the pervasive presence of medicine in modern life.

So, then, we should neither repudiate this art [of medicine] altogether nor does it behoove us to repose all our confidence in it; but just as in . . . agriculture we pray God for the fruits, and as we entrust the helm to the pilot in the art of navigation, but implore God that we may end our voyage unharmed . . . so also, when reason allows, we call in the doctor, but we do not leave off hoping in God.

St. Basil of Caesarea, *The Long Rules*, q. 55

For contemporary people, the medical professional is a symbol of great power over life and death. Many think of the physician and the pharmacist as if they are shamans or medicine men who possess virtually magical powers of protection against the demons of sickness and death. Some cling to every piece of news about breakthroughs in pharmaceuticals and treatments for diseases. These hopes and expectations are fraught with material and spiritual danger. It is not just that they are often unrealistic, but also that they make an idol of scientific medicine. At the root of this idolization of medical science lies the misguided belief that health and wellness guarantee happiness and a meaningful life. The therapeutic vision of salvation helps us to recognize this idolatry and its dangers, so that we gain an understanding of the true relationship, and the crucial difference, between physical cure and spiritual rehabilitation. It can assist us in ordering the goods of life appropriately and proportionately in relation to a compassionate, forgiving, and healing divinity.

Therapeutic ideas about wellness, wholeness, and fulfillment proliferate in our culture, and they certainly have found their way into the churches and the consciousness of ordinary Christians. Much too often, we receive and accept these notions uncritically, without sufficient reference to Christian teaching or sacramental discipline. Many of these contemporary therapeutic ideas are simply poor science, snake oils, like the popular diet plans that come and go. Yet, they threaten to displace what remains of historic Christianity's God-centered anthropology and vision of salvation. I suspect that if the vision of divine therapy were stronger in the minds of contemporary Christians, this displacement would not happen so easily, and ordinary folk would have a surer sense of the right balance between appropriate dependence upon scientific medicine and dependence upon prayer, as St. Basil recommended.

Divine Therapy

Cur Deus homo? *(Why did God become human?)*

St. Anselm of Canterbury

I write as a Westerner, of course, and in reference to the culture in which I was born and raised, although my Christian faith is Eastern Orthodox. Thus, I live with an existential tension as the two great Christian traditions — Western and Eastern — rub against one another in my consciousness. For, in the Eastern Christian faith, the therapeutic vision of salvation continues to influence piety strongly and occupies a central place in theology, whereas, since the late Middle Ages in the West, the juridical metaphor for salvation has dominated Roman Catholicism and also much of Protestantism.

In the eleventh century, St. Anselm of Canterbury famously elaborated a juridical understanding of redemption. He purged it of the idea of ransom, since Satan can have no legitimate rights over humankind. But he retained the central juridical notions of justice, law, and mercy. According to St. Anselm, the proper measure of the magnitude of Adam's offense is the dignity of the offended party. The result of that offense is human mortality and death. Because the party Adam offended is God, whose dignity is infinite, an ordinary human being cannot possibly satisfy this infinite debt. Only Jesus Christ, both fully divine and fully human, can accomplish this for all of humankind. Jesus Christ was without guilt by virtue of his sinless humanity, and therefore could pay the debt that humanity owed to God by virtue of his infinite divine life. Thus, mercifully, Christ was able to secure salvation for us all by his freely chosen and wholly willing death on the Cross.

Because the Latin church had assimilated the model of Roman law and jurisprudence into its sacramental and ecclesial life, Anselm's theory was bound to find a receptive ear. And, over time, its basic themes became the staple of penitential theology and popular piety as well. In Eastern Christianity, however, in the fourth century — long before St. Anselm was born — St. Gregory of Nazianzus illuminated the limitations of an essentially legal and transactional understanding of salvation as atonement:

> Is it not evident that the Father accepts Him [Christ], but neither asked for Him nor demanded Him; but also on account of the Incarnation, and because Humanity must be sanctified by the Humanity of God, that He might deliver us Himself, and overcome the tyrant, and draw us to Himself by the mediation of His Son, Who also arranged this to the honour of the Father, Whom it is manifested that he obeys in all things?[4]

Nazianzus did not specifically invoke the therapeutic metaphor here. Nonetheless, he set forth its necessary assumption: that human nature is in need of sanctification. Because our humanity is defective — because it is lacking in health and needs healing — our salvation requires a fundamental transformation of human existence. Salvation is not merely a juridical change in our status from guilty under the law to justified in God's sight (though it includes that). It is not accomplished just by the substitution or sacrifice of the wholly innocent God-man for sinful humanity. More important, a ruined, mortally wounded humanity needs to "be sanctified by the Humanity of God" in order to be restored to wholeness and perfected in God's true likeness. First and foremost, salvation is an ontological event in our human nature that re-establishes the "original" possibility; the inherent, ingraced capacity of the human person for unobstructed communion with God.

Since all have sinned and fall short of the glory of God, they are justified by his grace as a gift, through the redemption which is in Christ Jesus, whom God put forward as an expiation by his blood, to be received by faith.

Romans 3:23-25, RSV

Twentieth-century Russian theologian Vladimir Lossky sums up the Orthodox assessment of Anselm's theory of atonement in the following:

Anselm's mistake was not just that he developed the juridical view of redemption, but rather that he wanted to see an adequate expression of the mystery of our redemption accomplished by Christ in the juridical relations implied by the word "redemption." He [Anselm] believed that he had found in the juridical image — that of the redemption — the very body of the truth, its "rational solidity," *veritatis rationabilis soliditas,* the reason why it was necessary for God to die for our salvation.[5]

In other words, Anselm drove the limited truth that the juridical metaphor discloses too far toward a literal statement about the very existence of God and God's relationship to humankind. Anselm's theology is excessively cataphatic (affirmative or positive)[6] and rationalist.

Ever since Anselm, Western rationalist theology has theorized about humanity's redemption as a necessity of justice, sometimes quite literally describing it as a juridical transaction that meets the demands of the law. Often it has favored a forensic interpretation of redemption as simply a change in God's fundamental attitude toward humankind, God's proffered forgiveness or imputed righteousness, with little or no interest in the deep, ontological repair actually needed for our weakened humanity to be transformed into a true state of holiness and righteousness.

Supporters of these forensic theories of salvation have cited especially the letters of St. Paul, the letter to the Hebrews, and the Gospel of Matthew for support. In English-speaking Christianity, terms like "expiate" and "propitiate," used in translations of the Bible since the King James Version, have been invested with strict connotations of judicial punishment and payment of a legal debt, despite the fact that their Hebrew, Greek, and Latin counterparts are religious and cultic terms denoting pardon, reconciliation, and atonement by blood sacrifice.

The New Testament writers freely mixed and blended legal and sacerdotal metaphors because they understood that neither kind of metaphor completely captures the full mystery of salvation. Western rationalist theology, however, engaged in the dubious exercise of sorting the various salvation metaphors and sharply differentiating them in meaning. The legal metaphor became the special province of the virtually autonomous disciplines of dogmatic and penitential theology, while the sacerdotal metaphor was confined to liturgical and pastoral theology. A desire for "rational" theory, both in Roman Catholicism and in Protestantism, gradually forced the metaphorical and figurative imagination out of theology altogether. Rationalist theology found juridical metaphors for salvation far more amenable to its goals of conceptualization and analysis than medicinal and therapeutic ones. The juridical metaphor's definitions of God as lawgiver and salvation as justification and payment of debt also reinforced a heightened sense of divine sovereignty.

God is love. God's love was revealed among us in this way: God sent his only Son into the world so that we might live through him. In this is love, not that we loved God but that he loved us and sent his Son to be the atoning sacrifice for our sins.

1 John 4:8-10, NRSV

What if one instead follows out the strong emphasis of St. John: that God is love and his salvation is a freely undertaken, kenotic (self-emptying) service of compassion and self-sacrifice? Then the image of the physician and the metaphors of medicine and cure commend themselves to both imagination and intellect; for what do we seek more in the physician than compassion?

In his letter to the Galatians, St. Paul writes, "Christ redeemed us from the curse of the law, having become a curse for us — for it is written, 'Cursed be every one who hangs on a tree'" (Gal. 3:13, RSV). Into modern times, Roman Catholic theology and Protestant theology have interpreted this "curse" in mainly juridical terms, as Christ's voluntary acceptance of humanity's deserved condemnation to death under the law. Eastern Orthodox theology, on the other hand, has interpreted this scriptural passage, and others like it, in light of the kinds of Johannine statements cited above and the second chapter of St. Paul's letter to the Philippians: "Christ Jesus, . . . though he was in the form of God, . . . emptied himself, taking the form of a servant, being born in the likeness of men. And being found in human form he humbled himself and became obedient unto death, even death on a cross" (Phil. 2:5-8, RSV).

The Second Person of the Holy Trinity lovingly condescended to become a human being and, in perfect obedience to God the Father, willingly and with complete freedom, surrendered to a humiliating death on the tree for our sakes. By this "most wretched of deaths" (the Jewish historian Josephus's description of crucifixion), Christ rendered death impotent in his own body and thereby wholly sanctified our humanity.

The twentieth-century Russian theologian Georges Florovsky sums up this alternative way of understanding salvation in two powerful statements. First, "the death of the Cross is effective, not as the death of an Innocent, but as the death of the Incarnate Lord." In other words, Christ is victor, not victim. As victor, Christ turns the lethal instrument of the Cross into the medicine of new life for us. He reveals the dead wood of the cross as the tree of life and himself as lifegiving fruit. Second, "the Cross is not a symbol of Justice, but the symbol of Love Divine."[7] This theology of salvation wholly rejects the idea, which Anselm embraced, that God's mercy is conditioned by God's need to have his honor satisfied. The paradoxical nature of the Cross signifies that salvation is a profound mystery, a precious, impenetrable gift wrapped in the limitless, unqualified, and unceasing love of God. Salvation is not simply a forensic transaction that changes our *legal status* before God, but also a transformation of our *very being* that imparts to humankind a share in God's own Triune life.

In acute recognition of this salvific truth about divine love and its triumph over sin and death, St. Gregory of Nazianzus was moved to exclaim, "[Nothing is] equal to the miracle of my salvation. A few drops of blood recreate the whole world, and become to all men like rennet is to milk, drawing us together and compressing us into unity."[8]

All that creation is and is destined to become, all that humanity is and is called to be, is concentrated at this intersection where evil and goodness, hatred and love, death and eternal life traverse. "The world is created by the power of the cross, for God's love for creation is sacrificial," writes Sergius Bulgakov, "[and] the world is saved by the cross, by sacrificial love."[9] The sixth-century Armenian theologian David Anhaght ("The Invincible") adds, "He who laid Himself down did so on the Cross . . . [and] is still on it and does not distance Himself from it. And what does this signify . . . other than the everlastingness and everpresence of this holy sacrifice."[10]

We have set forth the greatness of the disease, let us also praise the Physician.

St. Augustine, *Exposition on the Psalms*, 103

Love is the only effective remedy for sin and mortality. Atop Golgotha, Jesus let pour his precious blood on Adam's dry skull buried beneath the tree, bringing him and all of his descendants back to life. Christ released the whole of creation from "the bondage of corruption" (Rom. 8:21, NKJV). "We needed an Incarnate God, a God put to death, that we might live," declares Nazianzus. "We were put to death together with Him, that we might be cleansed; we rose again with Him, because we were put to death with Him; we were glorified with Him, because we rose again with Him."[11]

"Sin burns the sinews of the soul, and breaks the spiritual bones of the mind, and darkens the light of the heart," writes St. Cyril of Jerusalem,[12] but Jesus saves us from these devastating effects of sin. He cures the cancer of mortality that otherwise spreads throughout the entire body and consumes it. Adds the twentieth-century Russian theologian

Divine Therapy

Paul Evdokimov, "The extent of evil can be measured by the power of its antidote. The sick are healed by a treatment that befits the stature of God. The physician, instead of the patient, passes through death and inaugurates his universal healing.... The cross is planted at the threshold of the new life — *vita nova* — and the water of the baptism receives the sacramental value of the blood of Christ."[13]

Sinning is an offense against God, but the state of sin is an illness that mortally weakens the patient. Adam's deadly sickness spreads to all of his posterity and corrupts the whole of creation. "Therefore, just as sin came into the world through one man, and death came through sin, . . . so death spread to all because all have sinned" (Rom. 5:12, NRSV). And, "as by a man came death," St. Paul elaborates elsewhere, "by a man has come also the resurrection of the dead. For as in Adam all die, so also in Christ shall all be made alive" (1 Cor. 15:21-22, RSV). Christ is the surgeon who removes the sting of death (1 Cor. 15:55) with the sharp instrument of the cross. And his body and blood are the medicine of our immortality. Mere "flesh and blood" cannot "inherit the kingdom of God," because corruption does not "inherit incorruption" (1 Cor. 15:50, NKJV). Thus, "this corruptible [nature] must put on the incorruption, and this mortal [nature] must put on immortality" (1 Cor. 15:53, NKJV).

In contemporary speech, corruption denotes an immoral or criminal character: a violation against morals or law. But its Latin root is *rumpere* (to break, burst, tear, rend, rive, rupture, break asunder, burst in pieces, force open), from which the English word *rupture* comes. In this sense, corrupted human nature is a broken, weakened existence, headed toward the ultimate disintegration of death, the complete decomposition of the human being. Although human nature is not naturally incorruptible, neither need human beings necessarily endure corruptible death. For God created Adam and Eve in his own image and likeness (Gen. 1:26). He built into the human being the capacity to transcend natural necessity, determinism, and entropy, and to grow in holiness, partake of the "divine nature" (2 Peter 1:4), and enjoy "eternal life" (1 John 2:25). This capacity for deification, to become like God, is natural to man and is in no sense a superadded grace. It belongs to the "image of God" (Gen. 1:26), according to which God created Adam and Eve, that they might participate in his glory. This image is the very essence of what it is to be human, and the power inherent in man to enter into communion with God. Christ restores the image to its full integrity and returns our humanity to complete health.

The serpent's promise to Eve that she and Adam would become immortal "like God" (Gen. 3:5) and "not die" (Gen. 3:4) by eating the fruit of the tree was not his to make; the promise was, rather, his proud pretension to godlike power. God made human nature compatible with his divine nature from the start. From the beginning, God intended that human beings partake of the divine life. The Word, who is the express image of God the Father, is also the divine archetype of our humanity. The divine Son became a human being, states St. Athanasius of the fourth century, because "He alone, the Image of the Father, ... could recreate man made after the Image."[14] The Word became a human being because the health of the image of God in humanity that was

Divine Therapy

ruined by the Fall had to be restored. Furthermore, God desired his created image to grow increasingly into the likeness of his own uncreated Being. Humankind must "mature . . . to the measure of the stature of the fullness of Christ" (Eph. 4:13, RSV), "from one degree of glory to another" (2 Cor. 3:18, RSV).

In Christ, a perfect synergy of human freedom and divine grace reversed the entropic process of human corruption and death. "There is only one physician," writes St. Ignatius of Antioch in the first century, "who is both flesh and spirit, born and unborn, God in man, true life in death, both from Mary and from God, first subject to suffering, and then beyond it,"[15] bringing incorruption out of corruption and life out of death (1 Cor. 15:52-55).

Jesus said to him, "Go; your faith has healed you."

Mark 10:52, REB

Soteria is the Greek New Testament word often translated as "save." It is a derivative of the verb *sōzō*, which means "to heal." The Latin equivalents are *salvare* (to heal) and *salvus* (made whole or restored to integrity). Thus, the words for salvation in New Testament Greek and in Latin denote therapy and healing. The Gospel writers take advantage of this denotative meaning when they record Jesus' healing miracles. An example is St. Mark's story of Bartimaeus the blind beggar (Mark 10:46-52), who enthusiastically chases after Jesus on the road from Jericho, boldly addresses Jesus by the Messianic title "Son of David," and earnestly beseeches Jesus to restore his sight. The New Jerusalem Bible renders Jesus' answer to Bartimaeus as "Go; your faith has *saved* you." The Revised English Bible translates this as "Go; your faith has *healed* you," while the Revised Standard Version reads, "Go your way; your faith has *made you well.*"

All three of these modern translations are "accurate." But not one alone captures the complete meaning of the passage. The healing miracles certainly concern physical cure; but they are not limited to physical cure. All four of the Gospels emphasize that Jesus' acts of physical healing are charged with spiritual and eschatological significance as well. The Synoptic Gospels (Matt. 9:1-8; Mark 2:1-12; Luke 5:17-26) tell the story of the paralytic whose friends carry him to Jesus on his bed, in the hope that Jesus will cure him physically. Initially, Jesus greets the man and, instead of curing his paralysis, announces, "My son, your sins are forgiven" (Mark 2:5, RSV). Scribes who are present accuse Jesus of blasphemy, saying, "Who can forgive sin but God alone?" (Mark 2:7, RSV). After this, Jesus does cure the man of his physical affliction. But he explains that he has done so in order that people "may know that the Son of Man has authority on earth to forgive sins" (Mark 2:10, RSV).

Many of the early Christian commentators employ this story to introduce the theme of the Great Physician, who redeems us in both body and soul. For example, St. Ambrose of Milan (fourth century) writes, "Alongside of healing the wounds of body and mind, he also forgives the sins of the spirit, removes the weakness of the flesh, and thus he heals the whole person. It is a great thing to forgive people's sins — who can forgive sins, but God alone? For God also forgives through those to whom he has given the power of forgiveness. Yet it is far more divine to give resurrection to bodies, since the Lord himself is the resurrection."[16]

The power to heal is the other side of the power to forgive. In the Gospels, this dual power of healing and forgiveness is a proleptic sign of the great restoration *(apokatastasis)*, when our broken bodies will be made whole, our sickened souls cured, and death abolished forever (Rev. 21:4). "By raising some and healing others," observes St. Irenaeus of Lyons in the second century, "the Lord . . . prefigures eternal things by temporal things, and shows" that he has the power "to extend both healing and life to His handiwork," so that we might also believe "His words concerning . . . [the] resurrection" that is yet to come.[17]

Those who are well have no need of a physician, but those who are sick. . . . For I came not to call the righteous, but sinners.
Matthew 9:12-13, RSV

My own Orthodox tradition interprets the original righteousness *(justitia originalis)* of Adam and Eve in the garden as an ontological condition, not a strict legal status. Before the Fall, human nature was sound and whole, capable of full communion with God. The first couple was in complete harmony with God and the rest of Creation. The ancestral sin brought infirmity and instability into human existence: moral sickness of the soul and death in the body. Henceforth, humanity is disoriented in the created world and shut off from perfect, unbroken communion with God. Therefore "our diseased nature needed a healer," concludes St. Gregory of Nyssa. "Man in his fall needed one to set him upright. He who had lost the gift of life stood in need of a life-giver, and he who had dropped away from his fellowship with good wanted one who would lead him back to good. He who was shut up in the darkness longed for the presence of the light."[18]

The Syrian church fathers used the word *mzag* to describe the "mixing" or "mingling" of human and divine natures in Christ. St. Ephrem the Syrian writes, "Glorious is the Wise One Who allied and joined Divinity with humanity/... He mingled the natures like pigments and an image came into being of the God-man."[19] In common speech, *mzag* describes a physician combining and stirring together two or more substances to produce a medicinal remedy. According to this meaning, Christ is both physician and medicine. As medicine of life, he is poison for Satan, but antidote for human sin and mortality. After he returns to his Father in heaven, Christ makes himself available to us through the sacraments of baptism and the Eucharist. In his poem *East Coker*, T. S. Eliot translates the therapeutic image of salvation into a metaphor of "the dying nurse" whose medicine for "our sickness" is "the dripping blood" and "bloody flesh."[20]

Divine Therapy

Nicholas Cabasilas deepens this theme of the sacraments as the medicine of life in *The Life in Christ:*

> Many are the remedies which down through the ages have been devised for this sick race. [Nevertheless], it was Christ's death alone which was able to bring true life and health. For this reason, to be born by this new birth and live the blessed life and be disposed to health, and as far as lies in man, to confess the faith and take on oneself the passion and die the death of Christ, is nothing less than to drink of this medicine. . . . Since the Savior had no trace of any disease for which He needed a remedy to heal Him, the power of the [Eucharistic] cup is applied to us and slays the sin that is in us.[21]

No infirmity cometh before the Almighty Physician as incurable: only suffer thou thyself to be healed; repel not his hands. He knoweth how to deal with thee. . . . Bear with him when he useth the knife; bear the pain of the remedy, reflecting on thy future health.

St. Augustine, *Exposition on the Psalms,* 103

God is spirit, and spirit is immortal, whereas we humans are physical organisms subject to death and personal extinction. The death that we die is not merely physical, however. The human person is a unity of body and soul. Men and women are physical and spiritual beings. In the first instance, Christian faith does not define death in clinical terms, as a cessation of brain function or a shutting down of the vital organs. Corruptible death is a fundamentally religious problem of meaning and purpose. Decomposition of the unity of body and soul is the demise of the human person created in the image of God. Human death is a personal, spiritual, and eschatological event of tragic dimensions.

Medical science is incapable of diagnosing the dis-ease of sin or of preventing corruptible death. Nonetheless, we live under the shadows of both sin and death. We are conscious of our mortality and the constant threat death poses of spoiling life and rupturing the communion of love. God's own image in us is liable to complete dissolution under death's sway. On this account, the Word chose to become a human being; willingly died a death that, in his own assessment, he did not have to die; and was resurrected bodily. To die with Jesus Christ all the while we live, to submit ourselves to his care and the sharp instrument of his healing cross, and to take the medicine of life that Christ gives to us as his body and blood — these things are not only the cure for our physical and moral sickness, but the source of eternal life.

All of humankind is the patient. Yet not all submit themselves to the physician's hand or accept his treatment. "Love does not impose the healing by compulsion. . . . Not all recognized the Lord of Glory under that guise of the 'servant' He deliberately took upon Himself," writes Georges Florovsky.[22] Some, however, did — and do. St. Luke tells us that in Athens, on Mars Hill, when the Apostle Paul spoke to a skeptical crowd concerning "the resurrection of the dead, some mocked, while others said, 'We will hear you again on this matter.'" And still others "joined him and believed" (Acts 17:32, 34, NKJV).

> Lord, have mercy. Lord, have mercy. Lord, have mercy,
>   Lord, have mercy.
> O all-holy Trinity, grant peace to the world
> And healing to the sick, the Kingdom to those at rest.
> Lord, have mercy. Lord, have mercy.
>   Jesus Savior, have mercy on us.
> By means of this holy and immortal and life-saving
>   sacrifice,
> Receive, Lord, and have mercy.
>
> > *Der Voghormya* ("Lord, Have Mercy"),
> > a hymn of the Armenian Divine Liturgy

Plate 1. Anastasis in the Parecclesion Apse Vault
The Bridgeman Art Library

Plate 2. Pentecost by Khatchatur
Walters Art Museum

Plate 3. The Annunciation at the Well by Gregory of Tatew
Scala/Art Resource, NY

Plate 4. Icon of the Virgin of Vladimir by the Moscow School
The Bridgeman Art Library

Plate 5. The Crucifixion by Barsegh
New York Public Library, Special Collections

Plate 6. The Baptism of Christ by Khatchatur
Walters Art Museum

Plate 7. The Harrowing of Hades/Anastasis by Khatchatur
Walters Art Museum

Plate 8. The Women at the Sepulchre by Khatchatur
Walters Art Museum

CHAPTER 4

Mother of God, Mother of Holiness

The name of the Mother of God contains all the history of the divine economy in this world.

St. John of Damascus,
Exposition on the Orthodox Faith, 3:12

Mary is the bridge from Old Testament righteousness to its fulfillment in the New Covenant. "All the sacred tradition of the Jews is a history of the slow and laborious journey of fallen humanity toward the 'fullness of time,'" writes Vladimir Lossky, "when the angel was to be sent to announce to the chosen Virgin the Incarnation of God and to hear from her lips human consent, so that the divine plan might be accomplished."[1]

In the previous chapter, we examined salvation, understood especially — but by no means exclusively — as the healing of our human nature so that, as St. Paul says, we enjoy "newness of life" (Rom. 6:4, NKJV). The Divine Word became one of us. He lived a life without sin, perfectly obedient to God, and died a perfect sacrifice on the Cross so that our corrupted human nature could be restored to health in him. Instead of death, he has made eternal life the human inheritance. In his "body" Christ brought us back to wholeness and holiness. But Christ "took" his body from a woman. Even the Divine Word grew into a human being in the womb of a woman. Just as a woman was needed in the history of salvation to bridge the old and the new humanity, the old and the new covenants, the Old Creation and the New Creation, so also a woman was needed in whom God might commence to render our corrupted human nature whole again. That is why the church calls Mary "the New Eve," "the New Mother of Life," "the Mother of Holiness," "the Queen of Heaven." The Orthodox and Roman Catholic churches, as well as the early Reformers (Luther, Calvin, and Zwingli), believe that salvation cannot be understood apart from Mary's role in it.

In Orthodox Christianity, Mary is commonly referred to as the *Theotokos,* which literally means "God-bearer" but is usually translated "Mother of God." In this chapter I seek to explain the theological meaning that title holds and conveys. Consistent with the practice throughout this book, I turn in particular to the hymnody (and, to a lesser extent, the iconography) that transmits the church's theology about Mary. It does seem especially appropriate that, above all, the church honors Mary with song, since it is she who sings the most significant song in all of Scripture: the Magnificat of St. Luke's Gospel (1:46-55).

Mother of God, Mother of Holiness

Men are men, but Man is a woman.

G. K. Chesterton

Echoing Verdi's "La donna è mobile," G. K. Chesterton remarks at the start of his fantasy tale *The Napoleon of Notting Hill*, "Men are men, but Man is a woman." Chesterton explains that he is referring to the "changeful, mystical, [and] fickle" character of the human race as a whole.[2] No doubt, even this explanation would raise more than a few eyebrows among today's readers. Chesterton is speaking of women in general. I take the liberty here to invest his statement with a particular woman in mind — namely, Mary. For if the church is right about human existence, Mary's sanctified life is a model of holiness and perfection for all persons, men and women alike, and fickleness could never be attributed to her character.

With the titles of "Second Eve" and "Handmaid of the Lord," the ancient tradition registers its firm conviction that the mother of Jesus exercised her freedom and made her choice to bear the Son of God with total sobriety. Whereas Eve asked no questions of the Serpent and was foolishly deceived through her passions by that tempter, Mary scrupulously interrogated her angelic visitor. Only when she felt assured that there was no trickery in his proposal and that this was truly the will of God did Mary consent to conceive and give birth to the Second Adam who opens the closed gates of Paradise (Luke 1:31). Only then did Mary pronounce:

"Behold the handmaid of the Lord; be it unto me according to thy word" (Luke 1:38, KJV).

No less important, from that moment on, states St. Luke, Mary kept all the things she heard and saw about the mystery of redemption, pondering them in her heart (Luke 2:19). In this light, we may say that Mary *is* the woman who teaches us that Man, meaning spiritually mature humanity (Eph. 4:13), *is* a woman. When, in the Epistle to the Ephesians, St. Paul speaks of mature (or perfect) manhood, he is reflecting upon the sanctification by which persons enter into the holiness of God: "Put off your old nature which belongs to your former manner of life and is corrupt through deceitful lusts, and be renewed in the spirit of your minds, and put on the new nature, created after the likeness of God in true righteousness and holiness" (Eph. 4:22-24, RSV).

Eastern Christian iconographic subjects take up this theme of Mary's holiness and special relationship to the church. Expectedly, Mary is present in festal icons about her life, such as the Birth of the Mother of God, the Annunciation, and the Dormition (or Assumption) of the Mother of God. The argument over whether or not Mary ought to appear in mid-Pentecost icons of the Descent of the Holy Spirit, however, is especially instructive for our purpose. It focuses us on important questions regarding the character of Mary's holiness — about the claim, namely, that she is the heart of the church's holiness.

Most iconography of the Descent of the Holy Spirit does not include Mary among the twelve apostles and evangelists traditionally seated in a semicircle.[3] Sometimes, however, Mary is present, and conspicuously so, at the center of the

Mother of God, Mother of Holiness

circle, an unchallenged focal point of the scene. In *The Resurrection and the Icon,* Michael Quinot objects to this practice. He maintains that it "relegates the apostles to a secondary position . . . [and] makes the icon of Pentecost an icon of the Mother of God."[4] Yet Quinot approves of the dominant position of Mary in icons of the Ascension in which she stands at the center of the apostles and evangelists. Here, he asserts, Mary is appropriately represented as the Mother of the Church.[5]

But why, one might ask, can't Quinot's sound justification for Mary's presence in the Ascension icons apply also to the Pentecost icon? Armenian illuminated Gospel miniatures in which Mary *is* at the center of the Pentecost scene seem to me to emphasize two important theological points about Mary and the church. First, they remind us that, like Mary at the Annunciation, the church is visited by the Spirit and thus enabled to give birth to faith and holiness. Second, they emphasize that Mary is herself the pre-eminent embodiment of the church's holiness, greater even than John the Baptist or any of the apostles.

A fifteenth-century Armenian illumination by the artist and priest Khatchatur illustrates this dramatically. In traditional Byzantine icons of the Descent of the Holy Spirit, the tongues of fire reach down into the apostles from the heavens (or divinity), which is usually depicted by a half-globe. (See Figure 1.) The apostles are seated in a semicircle at the middle level of the image. A center space in this semicircle is left empty. This is the space that Christ occupies invisibly as Head of the Church. In Khatchatur's illumination, however, Mary fills this space. (See Plate 2.) Also, the half-globe

The Melody of Faith

Figure 1. The Descent of the Holy Spirit by the Novgorod School
The Bridgeman Art Library

is missing. Instead, the tongues of fire form a dome over the apostles. Mary is standing, as an almost priestly presence, in an *orans* posture, arms raised and extended, and palms turned upward, indicative of prayer, or perhaps, in this case, reception of the Holy Spirit. This latter interpretation addresses the fact that Mary's head reaches right into the "dome" of the tongues of fire at the third level of this stylized three-story upper room. The whole is reminiscent of an Armenian altar set on a bema, or raised platform with stairs, beneath the church dome. The dove, representing the Holy Spirit, is seated on Mary's head and wears a halo inscribed with a cross.

Christ's speech to the Apostle John from the Cross lends support to this interpretation of the Pentecost scene: "Then saith he to the disciple, 'Behold thy mother!'" (John 19:27, KJV). The Eastern tradition understands this to mean that Mary is also the Mother of the Church, the mother of all who are members of the mystical Body of Christ. Sergius Bulgakov maintains, "The churchliness of the Church and power of entering into it are centered in the Mother of God, and those who have this power [which is of the Spirit] come particularly close to her."[6] Bulgakov's words call to mind the traditional icon of the Dormition of the Mother of God, in which Mary on her deathbed is in the middle, encircled by apostles and disciples. The Dormition icon is based not at all upon biblical testimony, but rather upon an early tradition that the apostles came together one last time in Jerusalem to honor the Mother of the Lord at her death. Like the Pentecost icons in which Mary is present, the Dormition icon emphasizes that she is the heart of the church's holiness. She is presented, even in death, as the first among those honored in the communion of saints. The Byzantine sticheron hymn for Great Vespers proclaims that Mary herself *is* "the Holy Place of God."

In sum, Mary is the Mother of God as well as the mother of the new humanity, the church. Paul Evdokimov writes, "The *synergy* of the holiness of Israel and of the Spirit culminates in the Virgin," and so it is by "the Holy Spirit *and* the Virgin's *fiat* that every believer is born again."[7] Eve is the old, sinful humanity's fleshly mother by whom death spread to the entirety of the race; Mary is the new humanity's spiritual mother from whom the only begotten Son of God remedied our mortality by taking her flesh purely, without corruptibility, and raising it to eternal life. "The Virgin's *fiat*," in Evdokimov's turn of phrase, makes it possible for persons to become her children, be adopted as brothers or sisters of her Son, and participate in his healed and redeemed humanity.

Our relationship to Jesus is not merely bilateral, as many modern Christians assume. Jesus has a mother whom he has given to us as our mother also. In like manner, my personal holiness does not belong to me alone. Holiness comes about in relationship to Christ and our Mother Mary. It is shared. Holiness consists in keeping and remembering what God has done in Christ through his mother for all of humankind. Holiness is a personal state of wholeness and spiritual wellness. But it also is an active virtue of service rendered to others, which Mary embraced by declaring herself the handmaid of the Lord. Holiness is ecclesial, entirely related and connected to the other great marks of the church: unity, catholicity, and apostolicity.

Mother of God, Mother of Holiness

While it is, of course, true that Jesus is every Christian's supreme model of holiness, Mary is nevertheless the first disciple and the first Christian. In her holiness she marks the path every Christian must follow. Jesus addressed the multitude on the mountain with the Beatitudes and then summed them up by saying, "You, therefore, must be perfect, as your heavenly Father is perfect" (Matt. 5:48, RSV). The words are Christ's. But it is no less a truth of the Christian faith that Mary gave birth to these words by willingly giving her flesh to the One who uttered them. Indeed, his birth depended upon her free consent and obedience to the Father. "The incarnation was not only the work of the Father and His Virtue and His Spirit," writes Nicholas Cabasilas, "it was also the work and will of the Virgin. Without the consent of the All Pure One and the cooperation of her faith, this design would have been unrealizable."[8]

"The Holy Spirit will come upon you."
Luke 1:35, RSV

The Holy Spirit descended twice upon Mary: first at the Annunciation, and second at Pentecost. The first descent was functional, for by it Mary conceived. It concerned her alone. She did not share it with others, except through the gift of her Son. Vladimir Lossky explains that "this objective function of her divine maternity becomes the subjective way of her sanctification." Lossky continues by pointing out that

Mary realized "in her consciousness, and in all her personal life, the meaning of the fact of her having carried in her womb and having nourished at her breast the Son of God."[9]

St. Ephrem the Syrian, in the fourth century, expresses in his "Hymns on the Nativity" an early tradition about Mary's conception of Jesus by the Holy Spirit. Much as the Only-Begotten of God the Father was born a second time of a woman, Mary received her second birth in having conceived the enfleshed Word in her womb. In a hymn Mary announces, "Son of the Most High, Who came and dwelt in me,/[in] another birth, he bore me also/[in] a second birth. I put on the glory of Him/Who put on the body, the garment of His mother."[10]

In light of these things, one can argue that Mary brought a special holiness with her to the Upper Room at Pentecost, where again, for a second time, the Holy Spirit visited her, though this time with others. "What degree of holiness able to be realized here below could possibly correspond to the unique relationship of the Mother of God to her Son, the Head of the Church, who dwells in the heavens? Only the total holiness of the Church, the complement of the glorious humanity of Christ, containing the plenitude of deifying grace communicated ceaselessly to the Church since Pentecost by the Holy Spirit,"[11] observes Vladimir Lossky.

No doubt the second descent of the Holy Spirit upon Mary at Pentecost affected her personally, even as she was in the company of others. Consistent with this, the ancient tradition conjectures that Mary was given the full understanding that she was not only the Mother of her Lord but of each person onto whom the Spirit descends. This is the reason why the church affirms the special place of Mary as Queen of the Kingdom of Heaven. One should add, however, that even with this high estimate of Mary's place in the scheme of redemption, Orthodox Christianity has not embraced a doctrine of the Immaculate Conception. It seems more consistent with the Gospel story that Mary, like the rest of humanity, was born into the sin of the first Eve. Otherwise, the importance of her humanity is diminished; she becomes merely a predestined instrument of grace, and the exemplary character of her achievements of humility and purity and freely pronounced willingness to be of service to God is less compelling. Nevertheless, it seems appropriate, if not also necessary, to add that by her birth-giving and motherly relationship to Jesus through the Holy Spirit, Mary overcame our sinful condition and became, by virtue of her special holiness, the mother of our salvation.

"Behold the handmaid of the Lord; be it unto me according to thy word."

Luke 1:38, KJV

Irenaeus, Bishop of Lyons, raised two important lasting Marian themes: the one of the New or Second Eve, and the other of the Virgin's *fiat*. In these, especially, rest the church's claims about her centrality to the Christian understanding of holiness. Irenaeus writes:

And just as it was through a virgin who disobeyed that man was stricken and fell and died, so too it was through the Virgin, who obeyed the word of God, that man resuscitated by life received life. For the Lord came to seek back the lost sheep, and it was lost; and therefore he did not become some other formation, but he likewise, of her that was descended from Adam, preserved the likeness of formation; for Adam had necessarily to be restored in Christ, that mortality be absorbed in immortality, and Eve in Mary, that a virgin, become the advocate of a virgin, should undo and destroy virginal disobedience by virginal obedience.[12]

Traditional Christianity interprets this obedience as the signature of Mary's freedom, not her servitude or a sign of weakness, as modern feminist critics have judged. The traditional argument is easily drawn from Byzantine, Armenian, and Syrian liturgies. However, permit me to cite a less familiar source of the early church. The fifth-century Syriac writer Jacob of Serug, in his series of homiletic poems on the Mother of God, takes up these themes of Mary's freedom and obedience with great imaginative force. In the homily entitled "Concerning the Blessed Virgin Mother of God, Mary," Jacob writes of God's respect for the human freedom of Mary:

> The holy Father wanted to make a mother for his Son,
>   but He did not allow that she be his mother because of his choice.

Maiden, full of beauty hidden in her and around her,
and pure of heart that she might see the mysteries
which had come to pass in her.

This is beauty, when one is beautiful of one's own accord;
glorious graces of perfection are in his will.

However great be the beauty of something from God,
it is not acclaimed if freedom is not present. . . .

Even God loves beauty which is from the will:
He praises a good will, whenever this has
pleased Him.

Now this virgin whom, behold, we speak of her story
by means of her good will, she was pleasing and
was chosen.[13]

There will be those who object even to this way of putting things. Mary's circumstance alone, they might argue, puts her in a subservient position. God and Mary are not equals, and God does the proposing, not she. Genuine freedom requires equal position and autonomy, which Mary lacks personally, socially, and religiously, they might add. This modern view, or some variant of it, affects much of contemporary Christian theology in a variety of expressions on dogmatic and moral issues. The subject calls for more attention. But suffice to say here that traditional Christian teaching is of another mind.

The dogma of the Annunciation is not the revelation of a

solitary and autocratic God; nor is the Annunciation a story of human subservience to that God. Mary is called to an act of *kenosis* (self-emptying, suffering love), imitative of her own Son's, even before he himself has revealed it to the world. For by conceiving the holy child, she risks humiliation and social ostracism. But whatever the Father asks of the mother, he asks also of his Son, who "emptied Himself... taking the form of a bondservant, and coming in the likeness of men" (Phil. 2:5-11, NKJV). This passage from Paul's letter to the Philippians is a reading for the feast of the Birth of the Mother of God. St. Paul argues that the kenosis of the Son of God lights the way toward a religious affirmation of human freedom and holiness. The true end of human freedom is voluntary self-limitation in loving service to others and to God. God holds to this law of love when he condescends to become one of us. Mary is the first human being to obey this command wholly and consummately.

So we may say that Mary's actions at the Annunciation foreshadow and complement the act of divine self-limitation lifted up and praised by St. Paul in his great hymn of the letter to the Philippians. As Father Alexander Schmemann has said, the Annunciation is about "the dependence of the Incarnation itself, of the Divine plan itself, on the free and personal choice of Mary, on her free acceptance of the Divine challenge."[14] And hence, and this is such an important and powerful insight:

> the divine plan and "nature" are revealed as focused in a free person.... Salvation is no longer the operation of rescuing an ontologically inferior and passive being; it is

revealed as truly a *synergia,* a cooperation between God and man. In Mary obedience and humility are shown to be rooted not in any "deficiency" of nature, aware of its own "limitations," but as the very expression of man's royal freedom, of his capacity freely to encounter Truth itself and freely receive it. In the faith and experience of the Church, Mary truly is the very icon of "anthropological maximalism," its *epiphany.*[15]

"Mary . . . is the very icon of 'anthropological maximalism,'" says Schmemann. What is the meaning and content of this term? First, it is not, as so much of modern and postmodern opinion holds, a matter of power. Mary is not "empowered" in the sense that persons have human rights and that, therefore, the marginalized, the impoverished, and the persecuted need to be "empowered." Mary's Magnificat is not liberationist in this thoroughly modern sense. Rather, it is profoundly *doxological.* When Christians give themselves over to God in obedience, they honor and praise him and become his holy people. Mary sings this praise in her Magnificat and announces the beginning of the great reversal from sin to holiness, and from death to life:

> He that is mighty hath done to me great things; and holy is his name. And his mercy is on them that fear him from generation to generation. He hath shewed strength with his arm; he hath scattered the proud in the imagination of their hearts. He hath put down the mighty from their seats, and exalted them of low degree. He hath filled the

hungry with good things; and the rich he hath sent empty away. (Luke 1:49-53, KJV)

A Byzantine hymn of the Annunciation states that Mary is "the Living City of Christ the King."[16]

Second, this "anthropological maximalism" does not mean "self-fulfillment." The meaning of Mary's holiness and perfection is not about the self filling up with experiences or possessions that supposedly enable the self to realize its own "potential" and obtain happiness. This was how Adam and Eve behaved. And we know where that got them. Blessedness, in biblical terms, is the self's abandonment of all such desire for self-gratification, as the human will conforms to God's will and God fills the person with his grace. To be maximally human means just what the church has said about Mary: that she is filled with grace. As Evdokimov says, "The human vessel proves itself worthy of the Uncontainable who takes His substance from this vessel."[17] Mary is the first to prove herself worthy. She is, as St. Cyril of Alexandria (fourth century) writes, "Mary, the ever-Virgin, *dêlonoti tên hagian Ekklêsian,* [is] the holy temple (namely) of God," the sanctuary.[18] Henceforth, she, and every person upon whom the Holy Spirit descends, may grow "to maturity, to the measure of the full stature of Christ" (Eph. 4:13, NRSV).

Mother of God, Mother of Holiness

Then said Mary unto the angel, "How shall this be, seeing I know not a man?"

Luke 1:34, KJV

Often I hear from my college undergraduates and in church parishes a description of the Christian faith as "blind faith," as if the height of Christian faith is to believe without knowing. This is an odd expression and an unfortunate cliché. It exposes a serious misunderstanding about the life of a Christian. Christian humility certainly demands that those who call themselves Christian not boast of their faith. Nonetheless, faith as it is found in Mary requires the believer to seek out God, to know God's purposes. Holiness is seeking to be filled with the knowledge of God in order to exercise one's own will in conformity with God's purpose.

Orthodox liturgies and hymns of the Annunciation emphasize this relationship of faith, knowledge of God, and holiness. For a visual depiction of these themes, see the Annunciation icon in Plate 3. Mary's encounter with the archangel Gabriel is dramatically cast in the form of a dialogue in which the notion that Christian faith or holiness is dependent upon an unquestioning attitude is dispelled. Mary listens to what Gabriel says: that she has been chosen by God to give birth to the great One whose Kingdom is without end. Then she challenges Gabriel with a series of questions. This is reflected in a cycle of dialogues that belong to the Byzantine services for the Annunciation:

Mary said to the Angel: "Strange is thy speech and strange thine appearance, strange thy sayings and thy disclosures. I am a Maid who knows not wedlock, lead me not astray."

"Thou dost appear unto me in the form of a man," said the undefiled Maid to the chief of the heavenly hosts: "how then dost thou speak to me of things that pass man's power? For thou hast said that God shall be with me, and shall take up His dwelling in my womb; how, tell me, shall I become the spacious habitation and the holy place of Him that rides upon the cherubim? Do not beguile me with deceit."

"O Angel, help me to understand the meaning of thy words. How shall what thou sayest come to pass? Tell me clearly, how shall I conceive, who am a virgin maid? And how shall I become the Mother of my Maker?" [asked the Mother of God].

"O Virgin, thou dost seek to know from me the manner of thy conceiving, but this is beyond all interpretation. The Holy Spirit shall overshadow thee in His creative power and shall make this to come to pass" [answered the Angel].

"My mother Eve, accepting the suggestion of the serpent, was banished from the divine delight: therefore I fear thy strange salutation, for I take heed lest I slip" [replied the Mother of God].

"I am sent as the envoy of God to disclose to thee the divine will. Why art thou, O Undefiled, afraid of me, who rather am afraid of thee? Why, O Lady, dost thou stand in awe of me, who stand in reverent awe of thee?" [asked the Angel].

"I cannot understand the meaning of thy words. For there have often been miracles, wonders worked by the might of God, symbols and figures contained in the Law. But never has a virgin borne child without knowing a man" [answered the Mother of God].

"Divine joy is given to thee, O Mother of God. All creation cries unto thee: 'Hail, O bride of God.' For thou alone, O pure Virgin, wast ordained to be the Mother of the Son of God" [said the Angel].

"May the condemnation of Eve be brought to naught through me; and through me may her debt be repaid this day. Through me the ancient due be rendered up in full" [answered the Mother of God].[19]

This is the story in a nutshell. And it is an interesting account that requires some further commentary. Jacob of Serug enters the conversation again, because although he cannot be commenting directly on these passages (they enter the Byzantine texts much later), he, like his predecessor Ephrem the Syrian, is certainly someone who inspired the content and form of these services.

Most important is how Jacob contrasts the character and

behavior of Eve and Mary. "Eve had not questioned the serpent when he led her astray," Jacob observes. She remained silent and fell to the guile of the serpent and his treachery. Mary, however, "heard truth from the faithful one,/nevertheless in this way she had sought out an explanation." Eve was told that she might become a goddess by eating from a tree but did not even ask how that was possible. Whereas, "the Watcher told . . . [Mary] that she would conceive the Son of God,/but she did not accept it until she was well informed."[20] Vladimir Lossky lends insight here when he observes that "scriptural evidence teaches us that the glory of the Mother of God does not reside merely in her corporeal maternity, in the fact that she carried and fed the Incarnate Word."[21] Rather, Mary's holiness has everything to do with her character. Nor is her virtue merely the product of grace that is simply infused in her in the same manner as she is impregnated. Her integrity and freedom remain. Her virtue is the sum of her intentions and acts. And as we have seen, Orthodox liturgy goes to great lengths to say that this is so. A synergy is at work because it is equally true that, as Jacob says, "God purified one virgin, and made her His Mother."[22] Jacob continues:

> She was pleasing as much as it is given nature to be beautiful. . . .
>
> Hitherto she strove with human virtue,
>   but that God should shine forth from her, was not of her own doing.

> As far as the just ones drew near to God,
> the most fair one drew near by virtue of her soul.
>
> But that the Lord shone from her bodily,
> His grace it is, may He be praised because of so much mercy![23]

Mary's supreme act of acceptance to give birth to the Son of God permits God also to translate her — and all believers, ultimately — to that condition "where Eve and Adam were placed, before they sinned."[24] We must consider the nature of Mary's faith together with the nature of her intentions and the disposition of her will. Her holiness is determined by the purity of her motives, by her discernment, and by the knowledge of God that she sought, gained, and kept in memory for the sake of the whole church. "For if Mary had not sublime impulses,/she would not have arrived to speak before the Watcher."[25] The wisdom that Eve sought for the wrong motives, Mary gained through her purity of heart. Jacob concludes:

> Blessed Mary, who by her questions to Gabriel,
> taught the world this mystery which was concealed.
>
> For if she had not asked him how it would be,
> we would not have learned the explanation of the matter of the Son.
>
> The beauty of the matter which appeared openly is
> because of her; she was the reason that it was explained to us by the angel.

The Melody of Faith

By that question, the wise one [Mary] became the mouth of the Church; she learned that interpretation for all Creation.[26]

"Yea, a sword shall pierce through thy own soul also."

Luke 2:35, KJV

St. Simeon, of course, speaks these words to Mary when he blesses Jesus at the temple in Jerusalem: "Behold, this child is set for the fall and rising again of many in Israel; and for a sign which shall be spoken against; (Yea, a sword shall pierce through thy own soul also) that the thoughts of many hearts may be revealed" (Luke 2:34-35, KJV). From the beginning, the church has interpreted Simeon's words as a prophecy of the great grief and suffering that Mary herself would endure as she watched her Son's crucifixion, death, and burial. This certainly is at the heart of the story of her holiness and how that holiness redounds to the whole church. Mary is the great intercessor because she has come nearer to the suffering of her Son than any other mortal and, according to tradition, was first witness to his resurrection. Her holiness is linked to the suffering and joy that she has taken with her to heaven, so that she pleads for the relief of the suffering of all her children, and for the forgiveness of their sins. A Byzantine hymn for the Feast of Ascension reminds us of this:

O Lord, having fulfilled the mystery that was hidden from before the ages and from all generations, as Thou art good, Thou didst come with thy disciples to the Mount of Olives, having together with Thyself her that gave birth to Thee, the Creator and Fashioner of all things; for it was meet that she who, as Thy Mother, suffered at the Passion more than all, should also enjoy the surpassing joy of the glorification of Thy flesh.[27]

There is not a trace of sentimentalism in this conviction. The redemptive character of Mary's suffering at the foot of the Cross, as she watched the life of her Son ebb away, and her great grief afterwards at the deposition of his body represent the struggle of fallen humanity against the temptations of rebellion and despair. The patristic writers portray a complex reception of Simeon's prophecy and, by extension, a complicated response of the Mother of God to her Son's Passion. Mary leads us on a *journey* to perfection. She herself is not instantly holy. She, too, like the full company of disciples, must pass through the scandal of the Cross and be purified by the fire of the Spirit. The sword foretold by Simeon is emblematic of the doubt and fear that rushed through the disciples at Jesus' capture, trial, and crucifixion. In his seventeenth homily on St. Luke, Origen comments, "What ought we to think? That while the apostles were scandalized, the Mother of the Lord was immune from scandal? If she had not experienced scandal during the Lord's passion, Jesus did not die for her sins."[28]

This is strong speech. But it rescues the veneration of Mary from shallow sentimentalism and insures that believers leap not too quickly to the triumph of Resurrection Sunday. Moreover, it secures a sober recognition of Mary's humanity — that, although she is given the name "the Mother of God," she is not removed from our human condition. The great sixth-century Byzantine hymnist St. Romanos the Melodist takes up this theme in his homiletic poem for the Feast of the Meeting of the Lord. He places these words in the mouth of Simeon:

> So much is the mystery contradicted that in your own
>   mind doubt will arise.
> For when you see your Son nailed to the Cross, O All-
>   Unblemished,
> remembering the words which the angel spoke and the
>   divine conception
> and the ineffable wonders, at once you will doubt.
> The misgiving caused by suffering will be like a sword
>   for you,
> but after this he will send your heart swift healing
> and to his disciples unassailable peace,
>   *the only Lover of mankind.*[29]

Here is the church's realism in its memory of Mary's suffering, indispensable to the Easter faith.

As mentioned, the Byzantine liturgies for all of the major Feasts of the Virgin Mary include a reading of Philippians 2:2-11. This emphasizes Mary's participation in the *kenosis* of her Son, especially his death on the Cross. In some icons of the Annunciation, Gabriel holds a cross to signify the same. And virtually all icons of the Virgin cradling the child convey this connection of Mary with the suffering of the Cross. Paul Evdokimov comments on the famous eleventh- to twelfth-century icon of Our Lady of Vladimir (see Plate 4), which poignantly expresses this understanding of Mary's suffering:

> Mary's face is elongated, her nose long and pointed, her mouth thin and narrow, her eyes big and dark under arched eyelashes. The eyebrows are slightly raised with folds between them. The fixed stare of the eyes looks off into eternity and gives the face an expression of a dense and gripping affliction. The corners of the mouth reinforce this sadness. The shadows of the eyelashes make the pupils appear darker, and the eyes seem to be plunged into an unfathomable depth, inaccessible to the look of the spectator....
>
> Christ presses his face affectionately against his mother's and is completely absorbed in the movement of tenderness and consolation. His attention, attuned to Mary's state of mind, is very visible in the focused movement of his eyes and makes us think of another icon, the Burial of Christ: "Do not cry for me, O Mother..."[30]

Postscript

In June of 1997, I was one of forty scholars and churchmen who attended a three-day meeting in Paris to begin planning commemorative events for the celebration of the 1700th Anniversary of Christian Armenia in 2001. His Holi-

The Melody of Faith

ness Karekin I, Catholicos of All Armenians (of blessed memory), was present, and on the Sunday of our departure, there was a Pontifical Mass.

I arrived at the church a few minutes before the start of the Divine Liturgy and was ushered in as a guest to the first row of pews. As I was taking my seat, a commotion arose in the church vestibule. I turned to see a young woman in a wheelchair being pushed down the middle aisle toward where I was seated. Her husband and her young son of perhaps ten years accompanied her. The mother cradled a small child against her bosom, and as I looked upon them, I saw that both of the woman's legs had been amputated. I struggled not to stare, but I could not help myself. Deliberately, I turned my head and looked up to the high altar. My perspective had changed, but shockingly not the subject. It was as if I was staring into a looking glass. Armenian churches do not have a Byzantine iconostasis, so that the view is unobstructed to the seven-storied altar. Above and at center there is always an icon of the enthroned Theotokos with child, and this is where my gaze fell.

Soon, another disturbance caught my attention. Someone hurriedly pushed the wheelchair to the side of the aisle to make way for the pontifical procession. As Catholicos Karekin I neared the woman, he made a gesture toward her as if he wanted to stop. This was not possible, and so His Holiness stepped forward and seated himself in the bishop's throne immediately in front of us. I glanced toward the mother and her child and saw the pained disappointment in her eyes. Some time passed before the Catholicos rose from his seat, came to the center, and turned to give the sign of peace. But he did not retreat. Instead, he stepped down toward the woman and her child, laid his right hand upon them, and spoke a blessing. The woman's face shone with a special light.

I do not know for certain how this young mother was crippled. I suspect that she lost her legs in the earthquake of December of 1988, which took upwards of fifty thousand lives in Armenia and maimed tens of thousands more. Nor do I know what kind of a life she lived before or after being crippled; I do not know whether she was virtuous or not. Nevertheless, she left me with a priceless gift: for as I received communion that morning, I was conscious in a way I had not been ever before of the presence of the Mother of God. I was thankful in a new way for Mary's compliance with the Holy Spirit's invitation to carry the Divine Word in her womb and to give to him her flesh. I was newly conscious of the affliction of the Mother of God and of her profound connection with her Son's suffering and sacrifice. The Eucharist and its promise of a New Creation in which we all are made healthy and whole meant that much more to me. Instinctively, I turned toward the mother and child in their wheelchair throne. But they were gone. They had left the church, the blessing having been given and received, the healing begun.

The ways in which God speaks to us and invites us into his life are as varied as the stars in the heavens. He may call us with the voice of an angel, through a vision, or in the fleshly presence of one of his children. On this particular day, God spoke to me through my crippled sister, who sat no more than five feet from me under the icon of her own womanly flesh and motherly love. I had at last embraced the Mother of our Lord as my mother and fount of holiness.

O Mother-of-God, tabernacle of the light of the unbounded sun of life, thou didst become the dayspring of the sun of righteousness and didst shed forth light on those who sit in darkness; wherefore we all praise thee always.

O thou undefiled temple and burning-bush who art not consumed, thou didst bear in thee the fire of the Godhead that is not burnt, wherewith the flame of the passions of our nature was burnt and consumed; wherefore we all praise thee always.

O thou living ark of the tables of the testament of the new covenant, through thee was cast up the way to the land of the promise, the Word that was fashioned in thee by the Spirit; wherefore we all praise thee always.[31]

CHAPTER 5

The Victorious Cross

I confess the Cross, because I know of the Resurrection.

St. Cyril of Jerusalem,
The Catechetical Lectures, 13:4

In Chapter 3, I discussed a theology of redemption and atonement that St. Anselm of Canterbury introduced at the close of the twelfth century. In *Cur Deus Homo?* Anselm reworked the juridical and penal metaphors with lawyer's logic into a persuasive "rational theology." His doctrine of the divine satisfaction influenced broad streams of Roman Catholic and Protestant theology. Aquinas, Luther, and Calvin also proposed their own versions of this doctrine. Thus, it should not be surprising that in our day, many Christians — Protestant, Roman Catholic, and even Orthodox — adhere to a belief in the Cross the lineage of which is traced back to these innovations, though the subtleties of their originating authors are usually lacking.

This piety of the Cross sees Jesus' crucifixion singularly, often virtually in isolation, as that action by which he secured our salvation. By virtue of his sinless life, complete obedience to God, and death by crucifixion, Christ paid in full the terrible debt owed for Adam's and all humanity's transgressions, thereby reconciling with the Father those who believe in him.

But this piety is fundamentally flawed, and it behooves us to understand why. For example, if one presses the logic of this contemporary piety of the Cross, the Resurrection (although it may be a comforting epilogue to the Gospel narrative) becomes unnecessary, for on Holy Friday Jesus accomplished all that was needed in order that humankind might inherit eternal life. However, most in whom this piety resides do not follow the logic that far. Although many espouse a conservative Christianity that fervently affirms Jesus' bodily resurrection, many also fail to recall the ancient Christian conviction that the Resurrection — not the Crucifixion — completes the purpose of the Incarnation.

Ironically, this piety of the Cross could not have come about but for the early church's conviction that the Resurrection is, indeed, the culmination of the Passion story. Over a period of forty days ending with his ascension, Jesus in his glorified body appeared before the disciples and a multitude of witnesses — according to St. Paul, more than five hundred (1 Cor. 15:6) — precisely in order to fix the truth of his resurrection firmly in the mind and imagination of a fledgling church. This is the significant narrative background of St. Cyril of Jerusalem's fourth-century pronouncement: "I confess the Cross, because I know of the Resurrection."[1]

The Victorious Cross

All creation was confounded with terror when it beheld thee suspended on the Cross, O Christ. The sun was darkened, and the foundations of the earth were shaken; all things suffered in sympathy with him who had created all things. O Lord, who of thine own good will did suffer for us, glory to thee.

Byzantine Hymn for Holy Friday

In the first-century Roman Empire, there was no glory in public crucifixion. If you and I had stood near the Cross, we would not have gained comfort from Jesus' suffering and death. We would not have walked away and confidently declared, "Jesus has died for our sins and saved us on that tree!" Something else had to have happened that removed the despair from his disciples' hearts and replaced it with hope. And that, of course, was the Resurrection.

From the standpoint of the ancient church's resurrection faith, Jesus was neither simply a victim of Roman injustice and cruelty, nor just a hero admirable for his teaching and for a life well lived. As Georges Florovsky writes, "Christ was not a passive victim, but the conqueror, even in his utmost humiliation. He knew that this humiliation was no mere endurance or obedience, but the very path of Glory and of the ultimate victory."[2] There could be no compulsion or necessity in Christ's crucifixion and death. These had to be undergone willingly in an absolutely free act of obedience to God, so that his death was a perfect sacrifice. Wherever sin exists there is no pure sacrifice. But Christ was without sin and could act without enslavement to it or captivity to death.

Christ's "choice" to go to the Cross was freely undergone, but not according to our ordinary understanding of "choice" as choosing between several possibilities or options. Neither was it the only "choice" he had. Christ chose to suffer and die on the Cross, "not merely in the sense of voluntary endurance or non-resistance, not merely in the sense that he permitted the rage of sin and unrighteousness to be vented on Himself... but *willed* it."[3] In the words of a fifth-century Armenian catechism, "[Christ] came willingly to death, and as All-powerful, was forced by no one.... Christ willingly, in his love coming to death, announced with a loud voice with awesome signs that even in death He was one in will and deed with the Father."[4] "Therefore, Christ as a man offered the spotless sacrifice to the Father, not intending to bring to the Father some juridical equivalent," says the Romanian theologian Dumitru Staniloae, "but to endow us through our union with him with the power of becoming ourselves a spotless sacrifice, so that we too might be able to enter with him into the Father's presence."[5]

Christ's death was not a suicide. There was nothing morbid or selfish about it. In going to the Cross, the Son of God chose life, not death. The movement of his will was in perfect accord with the will of the Father of Life, consistent with his unlimited love for humankind. With his arms outstretched, Christ beckons humankind to join him on his cross, which is at the center of the universe and on which life triumphs over death in his person.

The church calls the death that human beings die a "corruptible death" that dissolves the body-and-soul unity of the human person. Though Jesus' death was a real death, death's malevolence and destructiveness were exhausted on his divinity. His death "was an 'incorrupt death,' and therefore corruption and death were overcome in it, and in it began the resurrection."[6] The power of God in Christ rejoined body and soul and resurrected him bodily from the grave. What appeared, even to St. John and the grieving women at the Cross, as the humiliating demise of a powerless victim, was revealed three days hence as a conqueror's act of freedom, love, and power that overcame death.

He-Who-is-Crucified is He-Who-is-Resurrected. "He who truly died, the same is ever living," states the sixth-century Armenian philosopher David Anhaght.[7] Just as there is no meaningful distinction between God's weakness and God's strength ("The weakness of God is stronger than men"; 1 Cor. 1:25, NKJV), or between God's will and God's love ("By this we know love, because He laid down His life for us"; 1 John 3:16, NKJV), so the Cross and he who was crucified on it are inseparable. What looks to the world like weakness is God's power. God's love is the height of God's power. In other words: God's love *is* power and his power *is* love. "The One who alone is real has in Him as His own each and all the powers," continues Anhaght.[8]

Thus, the Crucifixion could not possibly have led to the demise of Jesus Christ, but only to his resurrection. For indeed, the power of the Resurrection is the power of the Cross. Henceforth, every cross is a crucifix, and every crucifix is the victorious Cross. *The Crucifixion did not make the Resurrection necessary; rather, in order that the Resurrection might come to pass, the Crucifixion had to be.* The aim and goal of Christ's suffering and death *is* resurrection. St. Paul proclaims that the power of the Cross *is* the Resurrection: "For though He was crucified in weakness, yet He lives by the power of God" (2 Cor. 13:4, NKJV).

O Christ God, who spread apart your spotless hands on the cross and gave us the sign of triumph, through it preserve our lives.
Armenian Canon for the Elevation
of the Holy Cross, First Day

When we view the Crucifixion in this light, it should not be surprising that the earliest Christian art depicts it with an emphasis on Christ's victory over death. The Resurrection shines through the Crucifixion in this *Christus Triumphans* type of crucifixion art. In it the figure of Jesus stands upright on and against the cross, his arms straight and outstretched, his feet usually set apart, his torso erect. His neck is straight or only slightly bent, and his eyes are open.

This contrasts with the more familiar *Christus Patiens* style of crucifixion icon that gained prominence after the ninth century and of which there are vastly more examples. (See Figure 2.) Icons and religious paintings of this type depict Christ in a wide range of ways, from a relatively upright, unmarked, and serene subject with eyes shut as if in sleep, to a scourged and bloodied figure that sags heavily from the

The Victorious Cross

Figure 2. Icon depicting the Crucifixion by the Novgorod School
The Bridgeman Art Library

Cross, his head fallen over and his eyes shut in unmistakable death.

We will consider this style of crucifixion in the form of an agonized Christ momentarily, especially as it has been presented in the immensely popular movie *The Passion of the Christ*, which came to the theaters in the spring of 2004 and aroused so much controversy over its graphic imagery and supposed anti-Semitism. I was dissatisfied with the film for different reasons. In my view, *The Passion of the Christ* is a kinetic icon that depicts the piety of the Cross with special force, which helps to account for the enormous appeal of the movie to a large swath of Christians across denominational lines.

But first let us turn briefly to the early *Christus Triumphans* type of crucifixion art, for it embraces a very different and ancient piety. This art unambiguously communicates the conviction and meaning of St. Cyril's bold statement: "I confess the Cross, because I know of the Resurrection." Let us look at two examples of this type of crucifixion art. The first belongs to the Syrian Rabula Gospel illuminations of the sixth century. (See Figure 3.) The second is an Armenian illumination of much later date by a fourteenth-century artist named Barsegh. (See Plate 5.)

The Rabula Gospel juxtaposes the Crucifixion and the Resurrection as a diptych on a single page. The Crucifixion is at the top of the illumination, and the Resurrection is at the bottom. In the former, Christ stands in an upright position on a central cross that rises high and stretches wide so that his unbent arms reach over the crosses of the two thieves on the left and right. His head is just slightly tilted,

Figure 3. The Crucifixion and the Women at the Tomb from the Rabula Gospels
Scala/Art Resource, NY

while his eyes are wide open as he looks compassionately upon the penitent thief to his right. Despite the fact that the Roman soldier Longinus is thrusting a spear into his side — according to the Roman method of verifying that the man is dead — this Christ is unmistakably alive. His posture and face express a quiet self-possession and radiant inner strength; in other words, peace and tranquility. The blood around the nails and wounds does not depict gore in a naturalistic way but symbolizes, rather, the loving and redeeming sacrifice.

The Resurrection shines through this crucifixion. This is emphasized by the placement of the empty tomb: at the center of the Resurrection scene below and aligned perpendicularly with the Cross. The guards lie asleep on the ground to the front and side of the tomb. In triptych fashion, two other Gospel scenes are depicted on either side of the tomb. On the left, an angel announces to the two Holy Women that Jesus is alive; on the right, the women kneel before the resurrected Christ.

At the beginning of the first millennium, Eastern iconography started to adopt the *Christus Patiens* model of the Crucifixion. Nevertheless, it retained important characteristics of the earlier *Christus Triumphans* form. Paul Evdokimov explains that this type of crucifixion icon "never shows the realism of exhausted and dead flesh; [and] painful expressions of agony have no place."[9] Leonid Ouspensky adds, "Everything which reminds of the corruptible human flesh is contrary to the [true] icon, for 'flesh and blood cannot inherit the Kingdom of God; neither doth incorruption inherit corruption' (1 Cor. 15:50), and a temporal portrait of a saint

The Victorious Cross

[or of Christ] cannot be an icon, precisely because it reflects not his transfigured but his ordinary, carnal state."[10]

Over the centuries, my own Armenian tradition has clung more tenaciously than even the Byzantine tradition to the inspiration of the *Christus Triumphans* crucifixion.[11] Thus, even as late as the fourteenth century, we find a rather remarkable illumination by the painter Barsegh that with the simplicity of a line drawing renders the distinctive *Christus Triumphans* form. (See Plate 5.) The primitive appearance of the painting is deceiving and belies a sophisticated theology. Barsegh seems intent on stressing the doctrine that the death of the Incarnate Word was not only freely willed but also incorrupt. Death exhausts itself completely in the immortal and incorruptible body of the Divine Word. Death is utterly defeated on the Cross and life triumphs. An Armenian hymn for the Feast of the Elevation of the Cross expounds upon the meaning that Barsegh seeks to convey: "God the Creator was lifted onto the cross, and upon it he renewed and revived those who had died in sin by eating of the wood."[12]

In Barsegh's crucifixion, Jesus' body quite literally blends into the wood of the Cross, as if he and it are one substance. As though he were commenting on this painting, David Anhaght writes, "He [Christ] who pleased to dwell on it [the Cross] did not depart from it, but dwelt, dwells, and will dwell there.... Therefore, the Cross is the Cross of God, and He Himself the Crucified One, God immortal, uncircumscribable and infinite."[13] The Cross and he who was crucified on it are inseparable. Christ and the Cross, his body and the wood, he and the Tree, are bonded as one and yield the fruit of eternal life.

Let me say a word here about the distinctive Christology that David Anhaght expresses so powerfully. While in this chapter we stress the victory on the Cross, this emphasis must not be at the expense of the suffering and death that Christ endures. This theology of the Cross strongly affirms that the subject, the person, who suffered death on the Cross was the Divine Word. God in Christ, through the flesh that he took from his mother, truly suffered and died on the Cross. This is the belief underlying Anhaght's insistence that Christ was "pleased to dwell on it [the Cross]" and will never disassociate himself from it. We can fully appreciate the greatness of Christ's victory on the Cross only if we also recognize the infinite love for humankind that he showed by taking upon himself the full force and malevolence of death, so that death might become a passage into eternal life.

In the Barsegh painting, Christ's elongated limbs, especially his arms that nearly cover the horizontal beam of the Cross, reinforce the impression that the flesh and the wood are one, and that the death that was endured on the Cross is taken into the life of God. The braiding of Christ's body indicates the suffering, and is virtually all that enables the eye to distinguish Christ from the Cross, his body from the wood. There are no visible wounds or nail markings on Christ's hands or feet. This idiosyncratic omission boldly emphasizes that the Crucified and the Resurrected are one and the same, namely, the eternal and immortal Word of God.

The two thieves in the painting are diminutive. They appear to be floating in space beneath this cosmic Christ. There are no city walls in the background; only empty space adorned with sun and moon, hung to either side of Christ's

The Victorious Cross

outstretched arms, as if he is holding them up. In the words of another Armenian hymn, "Today the Only Begotten Son spread out his spotless arms upon the Holy Cross./Most highly exalt him forever./For he triumphed over death by his mighty power,/and he called the universe to salvation and to eternal life./Most highly exalt him forever."[14]

Christ's eyes are completely open, as are the eyes of the penitent thief, whereas the eyes of the second thief are shut. Twice at the bottom of the painting, Barsegh carries over this soteriologically charged motif of open eyes. First, the eyes of the traditional skull of Adam at Christ's feet are open. The new Adam restores to life the old Adam. Second, just beneath this "living" skull, Christ lies in a sepulcher. His body remains braided, perhaps to remind us that his suffering is not something he leaves behind, but that it continues to bear significance through the whole of time and eternity. The open eyes of this entombed "dead" body may be meant to show that the Resurrection is already "happening" or "present," even in the grave.

Then he said . . . , "Ought not the Christ to have suffered these things and to enter into His glory?"

Luke 24:25-26, NKJV

Keeping the Rabula Gospel and Barsegh's crucifixion illumination in mind, we may turn now to the movie *The Passion of the Christ*. In an interview in the spring of 2004 with Mel

Gibson, who produced and directed the film, television journalist Diane Sawyer asked Gibson why he had depicted the scourging and crucifixion of Jesus so violently and bloodily. Gibson responded:

> I wanted it to be shocking. And I also wanted it to be extreme. I wanted it to push the viewers over the edge ... so that they see the enormity — the enormity of that sacrifice — to see that someone could endure that and still come back with love and forgiveness, even through extreme pain and suffering and ridicule.[15]

About the same time, Gibson explained to *Christianity Today* why in the last minutes of the film he deliberately juxtaposed images of the Last Supper with the main action of the Crucifixion. He said he wanted "to point out what it [the Last Supper] is, how it was instituted, and why."[16] In this way, he sought to stress the redemptive meaning of Jesus' suffering.

The Lord's Supper, or Eucharist, certainly does commemorate Jesus' suffering and sacrificial death on the Cross, but this is not all. From earliest Christianity, the Eucharistic commemoration has reflected the meaning of St. Cyril's proclamation: "I confess the Cross, because I know of the Resurrection." *The Apostolic Tradition* of Hippolytus of Rome, an early third-century text, includes a prayer of institution that incorporates this grander vision:

> When he was about to surrender himself to voluntary suffering

The Victorious Cross

in order to destroy death,
to break the devil's chains,
to tread hell underfoot,
to pour out this light upon the just,
to establish the covenant
and manifest his resurrection, he took bread . . .[17]

And all of the great catholic liturgies of the church do likewise.

According to Caleb Deschanel, who was the cinematographer for *The Passion of the Christ*, the movie's scenes of Jesus' scourging and crucifixion were strongly influenced by the sixteenth- and seventeenth-century religious paintings of the Italian Renaissance artist Caravaggio. In an *American Cinematographer* magazine interview of March 2004, Deschanel concedes, however, that Caravaggio did not depict Christ's wounds nearly so explicitly (naturalistically) as the movie did. Nor does he mention the fifteenth- and sixteenth-century crucifixion paintings of such artists as Lucas Cranach and Matthias Grünewald. Yet the crucified Christ in the movie strongly resembles the sanguinary and agonized Christ of these paintings.

Grünewald's crucifixion panel of the Isenheim Altarpiece (1512-16) is a good example and one that may be regarded as a historic predecessor of *The Passion*'s kinetic iconography. (See Figure 4.) It is a bold attempt to represent the human suffering of Christ on the Cross through naturalism in art. Grünewald uses colors and includes details in his crucifixion painting that are viscerally evocative of the agony of death and even of decay. Jesus' flesh is punctured and shred-

**Figure 4. The Crucifixion from the Isenheim Altarpiece
by Matthias Grünewald**
The Bridgeman Art Library

ded from the scourging and flagellation. His skin is a greenish, sickly yellow. The blood that covers him and is clotted on his forehead around the crown of thorns is dried and rust-colored. Grünewald leaves no doubt that this grotesque and tortured figure is a corpse. There is not the slightest indication that this dead body is the incorruptible flesh of the Incarnate God who will be raised in three days.

Yet Grünewald's crucifixion is not thoroughly naturalistic and modern. However grotesque the body of this crucified man, however tortured and expressive of weakness and not strength; defeat and not triumph; agony and not peace; nonetheless, Grünewald includes several significant traditional elements of earlier Christian iconography. Like his medieval predecessors, Grünewald alters dimension and perspective in order to emphasize Jesus' centrality and also, perhaps, his hidden power. Grünewald's painting retains motifs of a sacred cosmology and a sacramental vision of Creation, motifs that relate our visible world to a spiritual reality. This reflects the Christian belief that the Incarnation especially reveals this spiritual reality and has the power to clear even the eyes of those that have been blinded to it by the scales of sin.

Christ's perforated and utterly savaged body is larger than the figures in the foreground, emblematic of his divinity; his arms, hands, and feet are especially elongated. In traditional fashion, Mary Magdalene, St. John, and the Virgin Mary are positioned on the left. On the right is St. John the Baptist. The Baptist points to Christ with one hand and holds an open Bible inscribed with the text of the Gospel of John: "He must increase, but I must decrease" (John 3:30). At the bottom of the painting, a small lamb stands between the Baptist and the Cross. Christ is the "Lamb of God who takes away the sin of the world" (John 1:29, NKJV). The lamb faces the crucified figure and holds a cross, the sign of victory, and a chalice, emblematic of the sacrament of the Eucharist, the medicine of eternal life.[18]

But Gibson pursues historical accuracy with a vengeance and abandons this symbolism. If there had been no resurrection scene in the movie, the viewer would have been left with an image of suffering and a death that is pathetic, or, at best, the tragic defeat of a noble cause.

Despite the similarities in their art, Gibson's theology of the Cross is weaker and thinner than Grünewald's. Gibson strives to replicate what the naked eye might have seen, and that is all. Such naturalism does not even hint of a transcendent reality that lies "beneath" or "inside of" what the naked eye sees or the camera records. *The Passion of the Christ* fails to express what historic Christianity steadfastly maintains and traditional iconography affirms: that the soteriological truth of the Crucifixion and the Resurrection lies within the historical course of events and that the eyes of faith — or the eyes of the artist in this case — may read this truth out from ordinary reality.

In this respect, Gibson's artistry is entirely modern and thoroughly secular, not in the least sacramental, for it radically severs and separates the natural from the supernatural, the ordinary from the transcendent. Deschanel, who, unlike Gibson, does not profess to be Christian, expresses an opinion in the *American Cinematographer* interview that is revealing of the movie's modernism: "Of course, the story

The Victorious Cross

of this film is really pre-religion: it inspired a religion, but it's not a religious story. It's the story of a person whose powers come from forgiveness. . . . For me, it's [the resurrection scene] when the film becomes religious."[19] But if this is so, the integral vision of salvation in the traditional iconographic rendering of the Crucifixion is forgotten and lost.

My wife, my daughter, and I went to see *The Passion of the Christ* on Holy Thursday. I vividly recall my agitation and disappointment with the ending of the movie, not just the crucifixion scene, but also the resurrection scene. The hyper-naturalism that Gibson employed to portray the scourging, the nailing to the Cross, and the suffering and death on it could not work for the Resurrection. So he turned to a typical Hollywood gimmick: the portrayal of mystery as magic.

I was cognitively and emotionally jolted when the cinematography shifted suddenly from naturalism to Daliesque surrealism — to the aerial view of the crucifixion, the teardrop falling from heaven to earth, the burial shroud collapsing, as if the dead body disappears from beneath it, as the camera's eye moves to the figure of a resurrected Jesus seated near the stone slab.[20] This fantastical imagery of the resurrection scene does not connect effectively with the rest of the narrative, especially the crucifixion. Both the crucifixion and resurrection scenes of *The Passion* fail the test of serious Christian art.

One wishes that Gibson had taken a lesson from his sister in the Roman Catholic faith, writer Flannery O'Connor. She advised, "The novelist . . . if he is going to show the supernatural taking place . . . has nowhere to do it except on the literal level of natural events." For fiction "should reinforce our sense of the supernatural by grounding it in concrete, observable reality. If the writer uses his eyes in the security of his Faith, he will be obliged to use them honestly, and his sense of mystery, and acceptance of it, will be increased."[21]

O'Connor practiced in her fiction what she called a Christian realism, which is by no means naturalism. Quite the contrary, O'Connor avoided naturalism's denial of transcendent human freedom, as she also steered clear of sentimentalizing and trivializing religious mystery by depicting it as "otherworldly" and completely "outside" of history or nature. Christian realism endeavors to demonstrate that history and nature are shot through with God's purpose and grace. This is a sacramental vision of life that recognizes and strives to portray God's presence and activity throughout the created order. O'Connor writes her fiction as an invitation to discover oneself as a participant in a sacred, spiritual reality that sin or pride in the power of reason without faith blocks from our perception. As Dante writes in the *Divine Comedy*, "You who have sound intellects/Seek out the doctrine that conceals itself/Beneath the veil of the strange verses."[22]

"It is finished."

John 19:30, NKJV

In closing, let's imagine how *The Passion of the Christ* might have been made differently in order to represent persuasively the integrality of the Crucifixion and the Resurrection, and to overcome the deficiencies of the popular piety of the Cross with a truly sacramental vision of salvation by the Cross. I propose three key alterations.

First, the final resurrection scene would be left out. Instead, the movie would end with Jesus' final utterance on the Cross, according to St. John the Evangelist: "It is finished" (John 19:30, NKJV). Second, the movie would have an entirely different beginning. It would open with St. Luke's post-Resurrection story of Jesus' appearance to two of his disciples (Luke 24:13-35). St. Luke reports that on the same day that Jesus rose from the dead, he appeared to two of his disciples on the road to a village named Emmaus. The disciples did not at first recognize this "stranger" as their beloved teacher, though they were mysteriously attracted to him and were moved to trust him with their most personal feelings about Jesus' crucifixion and death. They also told him of the odd happenings that day at the tomb when "certain women of our company" found it to be empty and "had . . . visions of angels who said He [Christ] was alive" (Luke 24:22-23, NKJV).

According to St. Luke, when the disciples finished telling their story, Jesus said to them, "Ought not the Christ to have suffered these things and to enter into His glory?" and then expounded "to them in all the Scriptures the things concerning Himself" (Luke 24:26-27, NKJV). But even then the disciples failed to recognize him. When in the evening the company arrived at the village, the disciples invited Jesus to join them for supper. "Now it came to pass," continues St. Luke, "as He sat at the table with them, that He took bread, blessed and broke it, and gave it to them. Then their eyes were opened and they knew Him; and He vanished from their sight. And they said to one another, 'Did not our heart burn within us while He talked with us on the road?'" (Luke 24:30-32, NKJV).

The final alteration to *The Passion of the Christ* would weave this motif of the Resurrection, with its allusion to the Last Supper, into the whole of the rest of the narrative, like the gilt thread that runs through a fine tapestry. Gibson did include strong Eucharistic imagery in *The Passion*. But in my alteration, the Eucharistic theme would be charged with not just the sacrificial significance of the Cross but also the redemptive reality of the Resurrection, as a testimony to the truth of St. Cyril's statement: "I confess the Cross, because I know of the Resurrection."

CHAPTER 6

The Rhythm of the Resurrection

*"O Death, where is your sting?
O Hades, where is your victory?"*

1 Corinthians 15:55, NKJV

I was in Armenia. The electricity had gone off that evening. Kevork and I sat facing one another in pitch darkness at the small kitchen table with a single candle flickering between us. I leaned toward Kevork in order to hear the story he was about to tell.

"Kevork, you don't have to put yourself through this," I said.

"No, Vigen," he answered. "It helps to tell others what happened."

On a sunny December morning in 1988, the earth shook so fiercely in Armenia that the high-rise apartment in which Kevork, his wife, Anahid, and his two children lived crumbled to the ground. Kevork and Anahid had gone to work before the quake struck. But ten-year-old Armen and his seven-year-old sister, Lillit, were preparing to leave for school when

The Melody of Faith

the floor fell from under them and they were thrust into a black pit, buried beneath ten stories of twisted metal and stone. On foot, Kevork raced back home from the school at which he taught. Frantically, he began pulling chunks of concrete out of the jagged mountain of wreckage until his hands bled. When he realized the futility of his efforts, Kevork ran across the ruined city to reach someone with the machinery to rescue his children from their dark Sheol. But for three dreadful days, Armen and Lillit remained wrapped in suffocating darkness, removed from the land of the living. Through it all, Armen courageously encouraged his sister to keep hope. On the third day, the rescue team found the children. Two days later, Armen died in the hospital. His youthful body had been crushed from the waist down. Remarkably, Lillit survived, even though she had been pinned to the ground by a steel beam that lodged itself in her forehead.

"I have argued with God day and night!" Kevork exclaimed. "But God has not answered! Armen is gone! I will go on living my life in this sorrow, but I no longer worry about what God's purposes are or what he can do."

"Kevork," I pleaded. "You cannot mean that. Otherwise, why would you keep bringing this up?"

Mournfully, the heart-stricken father responded, "Vigen, my friend, what else is left for me?"

Kevork bowed his head. The ensuing silence thickened the surrounding night. Then he looked up and leaned toward me with his thin, sinewy arms, the arms of a man much older than his forty-five years.

"Vigen," he asked quietly, "you have heard of the Hare Krishna religion? My nephew brought me a book that I want

The Rhythm of the Resurrection

to show to you. There are drawings in it about the afterlife and the migrations of the soul. When I was a young man, we were taught in our atheism classes that Marxism is materialist and Christianity is spiritualist. If that is so, Vigen, explain to me what is the difference between what is said in this book and what the Bible teaches. Are not both religions spiritualist? I know that we Christians believe in resurrection, but help me to understand how this belief is different from what is shown by the pictures in this book."

"Kevork," I asked, "do you have a Bible?"

"Yes, Vigen, but it is a Russian Bible." Then he added, "I have a dictionary. We will make do, Vigen."

Kevork got up and disappeared into the darkness. Soon, he returned with the Bible, the book that his nephew had given him, and a dictionary that translated from Russian into Armenian. I got out my English Bible and my Armenian-English dictionary.

With these materials spread across the small kitchen table, in the candlelight, we commenced and did not cease until sunrise. Kevork and I read from First Corinthians and the last chapter of the book of Job. But here I am concerned with our conversation about St. Paul's First Epistle to the Corinthians.

"Kevork," I said, "St. Paul speaks of resurrection in chapter fifteen. Why don't you read in your Bible while I do the same in mine?" So this Armenian Job read in his Russian Bible, and I read in mine.

Slowly, Kevork read and reread the whole of chapter fifteen. His eyes grew wide and his lips moved rhythmically as he read to himself half-aloud. Then his face came aglow.

He looked up at me, and with a shout he exclaimed, "Vigen, Christianity is materialist! It says we will have bodies! I will see Armen's face again, just as I see yours now in the candlelight!"

What the Hindu doctrine could not promise this broken Armenian father, the Bible and Christianity did. St. Paul had assured him that he would see his son again in the kingdom of the Father of all fathers. It was promised.

Christ is risen, and life reigneth. Christ is risen, and not one dead remaineth in the grave.

Byzantine Canon for Easter

Kevork and I translated back and forth from Russian to Armenian and Armenian to English and vice versa:

> Behold, I tell you a mystery. We shall not all sleep, but we shall all be changed — in a moment, in the twinkling of an eye, at the last trumpet. For the trumpet will sound, and the dead will be raised incorruptible, and we shall be changed. . . . So when this corruptible [body] has put on incorruption, and this mortal [body] has put on immortality, then shall be brought to pass the saying that is written: "Death is swallowed up in victory."

This text is from the New King James Version of the Bible (1 Cor. 15:51-54, NKJV). Its rendering "O Hades, where is your

The Rhythm of the Resurrection

victory?" rather than the more widely used "O Death, where is your victory?" reflects the Greek (Septuagint) translation of the Hebrew Bible used by the writers of the New Testament and the early church and embraced by the Eastern churches to this day. St. Paul adapted his poem from Hosea 13:14. The Hebrew is rendered "O Death, where are your plagues? O Sheol, where is your destruction?"

Orthodox liturgy, iconography, and theology interpret "O Hades, where is your victory?" to mean that Christ's victory over death was accomplished not only on the Cross and by his resurrection, but also on Holy Saturday. Indeed, soteriologically speaking, Holy Saturday may be the most significant of the three days of Easter. On Friday, Christ is lifted up on the Cross. On Saturday, Christ descends into Hades, knocks down its gates, and liberates its captives — all of those righteous dead since Adam and Eve who died a corruptible death. On Easter Sunday, Christ rises again into the living world with his resurrected body. The victory over death that was commenced on Friday is completed. There is a rhythm of the Resurrection, like the breathing in and out and then in again — the breath of life. The *Christus Triumphans* type of Crucifixion iconography that we discussed in the preceding chapter echoes this rhythm faithfully. Through its imagery, it anticipates Christ's triumph over Hades and liberation of the righteous dead from that dark dungeon on Holy Saturday.

Corruptible death is death that dissolves the body-and-soul unity of the human person and breaks communion with God. The First Epistle of Peter states, "The gospel was proclaimed [by Christ] even to the dead, so that, though

THE MELODY OF FAITH

they had been judged in the flesh as everyone is judged, they might live in the spirit as God does" (1 Peter 4:6, NRSV). In the book of Acts, Peter addresses the "bewildered" crowd on Pentecost with these words: "He [David] spoke with foreknowledge about the resurrection of the Christ: he [Christ] is the one who was not abandoned to Hades, and [his] body did not see corruption. God raised this man Jesus to life, and of that we are all witnesses" (Acts 2:31-32, NJB). In Ephesians 4 (vv. 8-10, NRSV), St. Paul writes, "When he [Christ] ascended on high he made captivity itself a captive; he gave gifts to his people. (When it says, "He ascended," what does it mean but that he had also descended into the lower parts of the earth? He who descended is the same one who ascended far above all the heavens, so that he might fill all things.)"

On Holy Saturday, the Lord of Light and Life descends, this time not from heaven to earth but from earth into the "place" of shadows, into the pit of death. There he overcomes darkness with his uncreated light; overcomes corruptible death with his immortal life. On this day, the Godman, who is without sin and who reconciled humankind with God on the Cross, not only defeats death but rescues Adam and Eve from the pit of sin and corruption and takes them with him to the Kingdom of Light and Life. A Byzantine hymn announces, "Today Hell groans and cries aloud: 'My power has been destroyed. I accepted a mortal man as one of the dead; yet I cannot keep Him prisoner, and with Him I shall lose all those over whom I ruled. I held in my power the dead from all ages; but see, He is raising them all.'"[1] Likewise, St. Ephrem the Syrian proclaims, "By death

The Rhythm of the Resurrection

the Living One emptied Sheol. He tore it open and let entire throngs flee from it."[2]

There he beheld the dragon lurking in the water.

Armenian Rite of Epiphany

St. John Chrysostom of the fourth century reminds us in a homily on First Corinthians 15 that in baptism every Christian descends with Christ into Hades and participates in his victory over death, "for the being baptized and immersed, and then emerging, is a symbol of the descent into hell, and the return thence."[3] Eastern icons of Christ's baptism typically depict the waters of the Jordan in dark shades, so that the river has the appearance of a cave, reminiscent of Hades. Often a serpent or dragon figure lurks in the water. Christ, whom John the Baptist blesses, hallows the water and transforms it from a liquid tomb into the river of eternal life by his own bodily presence. The waters are once again the medium or amniotic fluid of life, the life of a New Creation in Christ.

Several miniatures that belong to the same fifteenth-century Armenian illuminated manuscript by the painter Khatchatur (whose Pentecost miniatures I discussed in Chapter 4) impressively illustrate this connection of Christ's baptism (and every Christian baptism) with Holy Saturday and the descent into Hades.[4] Juxtaposing the illumination of Christ's baptism with two companion folios lends not only a deeper understanding of baptism, but of Holy Saturday as well. (See Plates 6, 7, 8.) The first of these folios depicts Christ's descent into Hades, or the harrowing of hell, which I mentioned in previous chapters. The second represents the myrrh-bearing women at the empty tomb. Traditionally in the East, these two subjects represent the Resurrection, since the Gospels provide us with no description or explanation of the Resurrection event itself.

The three illuminations integrate mystagogical, soteriological, and eschatological themes. We will treat them as a triptych. Khatchatur employs typology and fulfillment, act and eschatology with as much nuance as any written theology. In the baptism miniature, Khatchatur presents Christ in a strictly upright position as John blesses him. (See Plate 6.) Like an arrow pointed downward, this figure draws our eyes into the water, where Jesus' feet pin down the body of a serpent at the bottom of the river. One foot is on the serpent's head and the other is on its neck. The creature is immobilized, and its snake-like body is twisted into a knot, emphasizing that Christ has confounded and thwarted Satan.

Khatchatur did not invent these details. They belong to ancient Christian sources. In this case, I believe, he reflects the great prayer of the blessing of the water in the Armenian Rite of Epiphany. A portion of this prayer states:

> And there [at the Jordan stream] he [Christ] beheld the dread dragon lurking in the water; opening its mouth it was eager to swallow down mankind.... But thy only begotten Son by his mighty power trampled the waters under the soles of his feet, sorely punished the mighty brute,

The Rhythm of the Resurrection

according to the prediction of the prophet, that thou hast bruised the head of the dragon upon the waters.[5]

The prophet to whom the hymn refers is the psalmist. "Thou didst break the heads of the dragons on the waters./ Thou didst crush the heads of Leviathan" (Ps. 74:13-14, RSV). Early Christian exegetes routinely interpreted these verses typologically as a prophecy of Jesus' baptism.

O Christ God, in the world-saving unfolding arms of your cross you gave us a scepter of power; through it preserve our lives.
Armenian Canon for the Elevation
of the Holy Cross, First Day

In the Harrowing of Hades illumination, Christ brings into Hades the divine uncreated light that presses out the eternal night of that realm in a receding penumbra like waves in an ocean of infinity. (See Plate 7.) He is clad in nail-studded boots with which he is trampling down a prostrate Satan who is trying to escape from the dark abyss. One foot is on Satan's neck and the other on his rump. Christ clasps a red cross in his left hand, like a staff or a scepter. The base of it is firmly seated on Satan's head. The Cross is transformed from an instrument of defeat and death into an unambiguous symbol of victory and a weapon that subdues Satan. Several verses from the Armenian Canon for the Second Day of the Elevation are even more explicit than the one cited above about the Cross as a weapon against Satan: "Christ, you gave us your cross as a scepter of power. With this, we shall triumph over the lawless enemy./This is a weapon of triumph, sharpened by the blood of the Son of God, and with this, we shall triumph over the lawless enemy."[6] The bright red color of the Cross could symbolize the Passion, as these verses suggest. But Khatchatur might also intend it to be an emblem of royal power. Last, as Christ subdues Satan with the Cross in his right hand, he draws Adam and Eve out of Hades with his left. Georges Florovsky argues that Christ descends into Hades in glory, "not in humiliation, although through humiliation" on the Cross.[7] This is precisely what Khatchatur conveys with brush and paint.

The image of the holy women at the sepulcher (see Plate 8) reinforces these themes of Christ's victory over the demonic powers and death by using some of the same color and symbolism that belongs to the other two illuminations. The angel announces the good news that Christ is risen to the women as he points to the empty tomb on which he is seated, and he wears the same spiked boots that Christ wears in Hades. The tomb itself is transparent, and inside there is a seashell, a conch, or burial wrapping in that shape. The shell is an ancient symbol for baptism. The spiral markings on it may also symbolize the womb from which new life emerges — in this case, rebirth through baptism in the Risen Christ.

With his spiked boots, the angel crushes the heads and bodies of three demons who are struggling to escape the nether region as he looks toward the three women in the upper left-hand corner of the painting who are entering the cave. Through a repetition of the symbolic number three, Khatchatur contrasts the scene of the women above with the demons below. By this same device he also lends dramatic effect to St. Paul's theme of descent and ascent.

In the upper right-hand corner of the painting, a risen and glorified Christ draped in royal garments stands opposite the holy women. He is perfectly upright, just as in Khatchatur's miniature of the baptism. Christ looks toward the women and blesses them in the trifold manner. In sum, Khatchatur harmonizes the Synoptic and Johannine accounts of the discovery of the empty tomb. He also adds details from the Gospel narratives and from his other illuminations in order to convey the singular Christian message of Christ's resurrection and his complete triumph over death.

In Orthodox Christianity, iconography and hymnody often are mutually interpretive within a liturgical setting. We gain some sense of the power of this combination and correlation of word and image, music and art, by holding in mind Khatchatur's illuminations while listening to the words of the appointed Armenian variable melodies and ode for Ordinary Sundays:

Melodies

The voice of good tidings sang to the women.
It sounded like the call of the trumpet:
"The Crucified whom ye seek is risen!
Fear not but be joyful;
Fulfill what is owed by Eve:

The Melody of Faith

Go to Galilee and see;
And proclaim to the world."

I tell of the voice of the lion
Who roared on the four-winged cross.
On the four-winged cross he roared,
His voice resounded to Hades.

The bird, the bird awoke,
and watching the gentiles,
He called, he called out to the turtle-dove,
To his beloved, nurtured in love.
Love is dawning, love is dawning,
In a stately march it is eagerly rising.
The rising sun, the rising sun —
Such is the name of that daystar.

Mary called to the gardener:
"Didst thou remove my first-born, my love?"
    "That bird is risen, the wakeful being,"
Did the seraph trumpet to the mother and those
    with her,
"The Savior of the world, Christ is risen!
And he delivereth mankind from death."

The Rhythm of the Resurrection

Ode

On the sepulcher of the immortal who is risen,
On this day the heavenly angel cried aloud:
"Christ did arise, Christ did awake,
Out of the virgin tomb, out of the tomb of light. . . ."
By the holy stone sat the marvelous one and cried aloud,
And the oil-bearing women announced joyfully:
"Christ did arise, Christ did awake,
Out of the new tomb, out of the virgin tomb."[8]

The "new song" of the kingdom has commenced. It sings of Christ's triumph over death on the Cross and in the depths of Hades, his resurrection, and the gift of eternal life in a New Creation.

By thy burial we are set free from death.

Byzantine Matins for Holy Saturday

In his commentary on the Nicene Creed, Father Alexander Schmemann writes, "We instinctively ask ourselves: why is this word [buried] used, and not the word 'died'?"[9] The Creed states: "And he was . . . crucified and suffered and was buried." Schmemann proposes that burial is "an affirmation of a particular understanding of death." In the Christian faith, burial points to things and actions that occur after death. In the case of the death of Jesus Christ, this means

"He, who is life itself, descends to death out of love and co-suffering, descends to a death which he did not create, which has taken over the world and poisoned life."[10] The Life of life dies willingly in order to overcome mortality and corruptible death. The New Adam rescues us from the condition of mortality in which the Old Adam's sin left us. The Son of God brings light, his own uncreated, immaterial light, to the dead who are covered in darkness and subject to the worm. And when he "raised up the dead from the dwelling place beneath the earth, all the powers of heaven cried aloud: 'Giver of Life, O Christ, glory to Thee.'"[11]

In a Byzantine hymn for Holy Saturday, Christ speaks from out of the tomb to comfort his mother and the other women who visit his dead body in the morning:

> By mine own will this earth covers Me, O Mother, but the gatekeepers of hell tremble as they see Me, clothed in the bloodstained garment of vengeance: for on the Cross as God have I struck down Mine enemies, and I shall rise again....
>
> Let the creation rejoice exceedingly, let all those born on earth be glad: for hell, the enemy, has been despoiled. Ye women, come to meet Me with sweet spices: for I am delivering Adam and Eve with all their offspring, and on the third day I will rise again.[12]

This is the One who also announces to the seer of the book of Revelation, "Do not be afraid; I am the First and the Last. I am He who lives, and was dead, and behold, I am alive forevermore. Amen. And I have the keys of Hades and of Death" (Rev. 1:17-18, NKJV).

In other religions, death is greeted as the immortal soul's great liberator from earthly captivity and woe. In the Christian faith, however, death is the great despoiler of the creature whom God has made in his very own image, whom he has made for eternal life. The human person is not just a soul, for then he is a ghost; nor is he simply a physical body, for then he is a corpse. The human person is a body-and-soul unity, and death sunders this unity. This is the meaning of the corruption of which St. Paul speaks. And it is this death to which my friend Kevork sought an answer. His own flesh and blood had been crushed under concrete and steel, and he yearned to see and embrace that flesh and blood once again.

St. Paul promised what the Hare Krishna religion could not: that the dead person would be made whole again. Not that the soul would go on existing in some other disembodied form in some nebulous netherworld, but that this very same "corruptible [body would] put on incorruption, and this mortal [body would] put on immortality" (1 Cor. 15:53, NKJV). "If men's bodies are to be detained in the earth," writes St. John Chrysostom, "it follows that the tyranny of death remains.... But if this, which Paul spoke of, ensues, as undoubtedly it will ensue, God's victory will appear, and that a glorious one, in His being able to raise again the bodies which were hidden thereby."[13]

From his reading of First Corinthians, my friend Kevork grasped this Christian truth about the promise of resurrection, and he greeted it with a shout of joy. I often tell the story of that night of discovery and revelation to my college students. I do so because of the profound confusion about Christian belief that so many of them carry about. Many who regard themselves as Christians do not comprehend or believe what Kevork hoped for, discovered, and rejoiced in. Many do not believe in the resurrection of the body. As Schmemann astutely observes, "In the real life of contemporary Christianity and Christians, faith in the resurrection has very little place, however strange that may sound." Ask a contemporary churchgoer what he or she really thinks about death, and "you will hear some vague, and still pre-Christian, idea about the immortality of the soul and its life in some sort of world beyond the grave."[14] This Christian may even affirm that Christ rose bodily and still believe that what awaits us is an immortal existence of the soul.

The Orthodox theology of Holy Saturday rights that error in an unexpected but powerful way. Christ's post-resurrection appearances, especially his encounter with the doubting Thomas, have been invoked countless times to correct neo-Hellenization of the Christian faith. These stories are about Christ and about his resurrected body. Holy Saturday, however, is about our destinies. Hades is a place of dread because it is a "place of... disembodiment and disincarnation,"[15] a shadowy, insubstantial, spectral realm. Christ's descent into Hades is the pre-condition not only of his own bodily resurrection, but of ours as well.[16]

On Holy Saturday, Hades is abolished once and for all. Through the mythopoeic imagery of the Bible, and of Christian liturgy and art, we grasp that corruptible, disincarnate death is not our ultimate fate. Instead, our fate is bodily resurrection and eternal life, whether with God or separated from him. As Georges Florovsky tersely states, "The descent into hell [Hades] is already the resurrection."[17]

Jesus Christ's death was a real human death. But as I pointed out in the last chapter, Christ did not have to die because, unlike all of the rest of humankind, he was without sin. For this reason also, his death was not corruptible: his body did not decay in the grave. By an act of infinite, redeeming love, the incarnate Word, the immortal Lord of life, accepted death freely and willingly and overcame corruptible death in his body and in our body — through the humanity that he took from his mother, which he bore with him on the Cross and took back to his Father in heaven.

When Jesus died on the Cross, his body and soul were separated. Thus he died just the sort of death to which all of humankind is subject. Nevertheless, body and soul continued in unbroken communication through the power of the Hypostatic Union[18] so that there was no corruption in Jesus' death. St. Gregory of Nyssa explains: "When our nature, following its own proper course, had even in Him been advanced to the separation of soul and body, He knitted together again the disunited elements, cementing them, as it were, together with the cement of His divine power, and recombining what has been severed in a reunion never to be broken. And this is the Resurrection."[19]

Death did not separate Christ from the enlivening love of the Father and the Holy Spirit, and even though his body and soul were separated topically (i.e., by location), they remained hypostatically "united through the Word."[20] A Paschal hymn of the Orthodox Church declares, "In the Grave with the body, and in Hades with the soul, in that thou art God; in Paradise with the thief, and on the throne with the Father and the Spirit, in that thou art infinite."[21] Despite the fact that Jesus dies, his divine Hypostasis (Person) remains incarnate. He who descends into Hades and ascends to the Father is the very same being who was born of the Virgin Mary, was crucified, died, and was buried. We narrate these "events" in terms of a temporal chronology. Yet, in truth, Christ simultaneously descends into Hades and lies bodily in the grave; is present with the thief in Paradise; and is on the throne with the Father and the Spirit. Time is transformed in Christ's deified body. With him we participate in eternity. That is how Christians are able to say that the Son who is present through the power of the Spirit in the elements at the Eucharistic table is also with the Father in heaven. In truth, even at this very "moment," Christ is liberating souls from Hades and accomplishing his resurrection and theirs.

The last enemy to be destroyed is death.

1 Corinthians 15:26, RSV

With the rising of the sun came a new day during which Kevork drove me to Armen's grave. Printed on the great polished granite stone was a nearly life-sized photograph of Armen. Kevork dropped to his knees in prayer, and then, with a care so intense that it created its own dense atmo-

The Rhythm of the Resurrection

sphere, as incense at the altar, he slowly, reverently wiped the whole surface of the gravestone with a new white handkerchief. The polished stone shone bright in the noonday sun, and the father, his eyes washed in tears, sighed a deep sigh.

I looked around me at all of the other new gravestones. Leninakan — which today has been returned to its ancient name of Giumri — was a city of some two hundred thousand when the earthquake struck. More than fifteen thousand persons perished when the earth trembled on that December day. Their gravestones populate whole hillsides — entire families buried next to one another — a city of the dead, waiting, waiting for the sound of the trumpet, the last call, and the Resurrection. What does St. Paul say? "For the trumpet will sound, and the dead will be raised incorruptible, and we shall be changed" (1 Cor. 15:52, NKJV). But what kind of a hope is this, this resurrection hope, if not something more than the hope of my own individual immortality? What good would such immortality be without the presence of the others whom I loved in life and who loved me?

As I looked out on this city of graves, I began to realize in my gut, and not just my intellect, that Holy Saturday has a profound social meaning. Through its symbolism of the victory of Christ over death, commemorated liturgically, the Resurrection is revealed as a communal event. Christ's descent into Hades is a triumph over the desolation and the loneliness, the isolation and the despair, that Satan, sin, and death have inflicted upon every human being.

In a wonderful study of Eastern iconography entitled,

simply enough, *The Art of the Icon: A Theology of Beauty,* Paul Evdokimov discusses a fourteenth-century painting of the descent into Hades that still exists in the chapel of the Church of the Holy Savior of Chora in Constantinople. (See Plate 1.) It is a painting filled with persons and movement. And it dramatically portrays this social character of the Christian belief in the Resurrection. Evdokimov writes:

> In a powerful hand movement, Christ yanks bewildered Adam and Eve from Hades. We have here the *powerful meeting of the two Adams* and a foretelling of the fullness of the Kingdom. The two Adams are together and identify one another, no longer in the *kenosis* of the Incarnation, but in the Glory of the Parousia. He who said to Adam "Where are you?" has mounted the Cross to search for him who was lost. He went down into Hades saying: "Come to me, my image and likeness" (a hymn by St. Ephrem). This is why the groups on the left and the right are in the background: they are the constitutive elements of Adam — that is, all humanity, individual men and women. They are the righteous and the prophets. On the left are the kings David and Solomon; they are preceded by the Forerunner, whose gesture calls attention and points to the Savior. On the right is Moses, who often carries the Tablets of the Law. All recognize the Savior and express their recognition by their gestures and attitudes.[22]

"True heavenly bliss is impossible for me if I isolate myself from the world-whole and care about myself only,"

The Rhythm of the Resurrection

wrote the great twentieth-century Russian religious philosopher Nicholas Berdyaev.[23] Satan prompts us to act this way and seals our fate in desolation. Were it not for the Son of God's victory over sin and death, this might be our fate. If Hades is the shadow of isolation and desolation cast by sin, then Christ's descent into Hades and his rescue of its inhabitants is the deed by which he begins the reunion of all who truly repent and believe in him within the Kingdom of Love. A prayer of the Armenian burial service poignantly expresses this hope and expectation: "Our Father ... thou hast vouchsafed unto us a place of rest from our earthly toils, the painless and the toilless life. Thou through thy only-begotten Son hast slain death and hast illumined this life and incorruptibility. And thou hast saved the holy ones from the dominion of darkness, and hast transferred them to the kingdom of thy beloved Son our Lord and Savior Jesus Christ."[24]

This final victory over death that St. Paul proclaims is a triumph of communion over isolation, and of love over desolation. "To earth Thou didst come down, O master, to save Adam: and not finding him on earth, Thou hast descended into hell, seeking him there.... Uplifted on the Cross, Thou hast uplifted with Thyself all living men; and then descending beneath the earth, Thou raisest all that lie buried there."[25]

In the evening, there was a humble supper at Kevork's home. Family and friends gathered. We cooked kebab on a grill, while others brought sweets and drink. It was not the great wedding feast. But it *was* a foretaste of that heavenly banquet. Even amidst the sorrows of our greatest losses in life, God permits us to taste of the kingdom of heaven. In his magnificent catechetical address, which is repeated at every Byzantine Easter matins service, St. John Chrysostom proclaims:

> Enter you all into the joy of your Lord; and receive your reward....
> The table is full-laden; feast you all sumptuously. Enjoy you all the feast of faith: Receive you all the riches of loving-kindness.... Let no one fear death, for the savior's death hath set us free.... O Death, where is thy sting? O Hell, where is thy victory? Christ is risen, and thou art overthrown. Christ is risen, and the demons are fallen. Christ is risen, and the Angels rejoice. Christ is risen, and life reigneth. Christ is risen, and not one dead remaineth in the grave.[26]

This truly is the eighth day and the first day of the New Creation.

NOTES

Notes to the Preface

1. I do not discount the possibility that music may even be "prehuman," as in the case of the bird songs I am hearing through my open windows this morning. It is no less valid to ascribe color and repetition to these sounds than it is to identify color and repetition in the plumage of the birds that sing them.

2. Sir Thomas Browne, *The Religio Medici and Other Writings* (London: J. M. Dent & Sons, 1940), p. 80.

3. Justin Martyr, "The First Apology of Justin," in *The Ante-Nicene Fathers*, vol. 1 (Grand Rapids: Wm. B. Eerdmans, 1996), p. 166.

4. Caius, "Against the Heresy of Artemon," as cited in Eusebius's *Ecclesiastical History*, vol. 28, in *The Ante-Nicene Fathers*, vol. 5 (Buffalo, N.Y.: The Christian Literature Publishing Company, 1886), p. 601.

5. Philip Sherrard, *The Sacred in Life and Art* (Evia, Greece: Denise Harvey, Publisher, 2004), p. 72.

6. Andrew Louth, "Orthodoxy and Art," in *Living Orthodoxy in the Modern World*, ed. Andrew Walker and Costa Carras (Crestwood, N.Y.: St. Vladimir's Seminary Press, 2000), pp. 166-67.

7. *The Early Christian Hymn Book: The Odes of Solomon*, trans. James H. Charlesworth (Eugene, Ore.: Cascade Books, 2009), p. 13.

8. Jaroslav Pelikan, *The Melody of Theology* (Cambridge, Mass.: Harvard University Press, 1988), p. ix.

9. Alexander Schmemann, *The Journals of Father Alexander Schmemann, 1973-1983*, trans. Juliana Schmemann (Crestwood, N.Y.: St. Vladimir's Seminary Press, 2000), p. 9.

Notes to Chapter 1

1. John of Kronstadt, cited by Kallistos Ware in *The Orthodox Way*, rev. ed. (Crestwood, N.Y.: St. Vladimir's Seminary Press, 1995), p. 44.
2. Fyodor Dostoevsky, *The Brothers Karamazov*, trans. Richard Pevear and Larissa Volokhonsky (New York: Farrar, Straus and Giroux, 2002), p. 592.
3. Douglas H. Knight, *The Eschatological Economy* (Grand Rapids: Wm. B. Eerdmans, 2006), p. 149.
4. Gregory of Nyssa, *Commentary on the Inscriptions on the Psalms*, trans. Casimir McCambley, O.C.S.O. (Brookline, Mass.: Hellenic College Press, 1999), p. 28.
5. *The Book of Hours of the Order of Common Prayer of the Armenian Apostolic Orthodox Church*, trans. Tiran Nersoyan (Evanston, Ill.: Ouzoonian House, 1994), p. 32.
6. Gregory of Nyssa, *Commentary on the Inscriptions on the Psalms*, pp. 28, 29.
7. Basil of Caesarea, *Hexaemeron*, in *St Basil: Letters and Select Works*, in *A Select Library of the Nicene and Post-Nicene Fathers of the Christian Church*, 2d series, vol. 8 (Grand Rapids: Wm. B. Eerdmans, 1996), p. 55.
8. Ware, *The Orthodox Way*, p. 45.
9. St. Philaret, as quoted in Vladimir Lossky, *The Mystical Theology of the Eastern Church* (Crestwood, N.Y.: St. Vladimir's Seminary Press, 1976), p. 92.
10. Gregory of Nazianzus, "Concerning the World," in *On God and Man: The Theological Poetry of St. Gregory of Nazianzus* (Crestwood, N.Y.: St. Vladimir's Seminary Press, 2001), p. 51.
11. William Faulkner, *The Sound and the Fury* (New York: Random House, 1984), p. 97.

12. The Cappadocian Fathers of the fourth century spoke of God the Father as "cause" of the Son whom he begets and of the Holy Spirit whom he breathes forth and also the "cause" of the unity of the three Persons as one Divinity. But this is a special use of language. It certainly is not causality in the ordinary philosophical or scientific senses of the word wherein cause is superior to effect. The eternal love of the Father is the hypostatization (personalization) of the Godhead as Father, Son, and Holy Spirit — one God. The Son and the Holy Spirit are neither subordinate to nor lesser in being than the Father. And there is not an extraposition of cause and effect, or a temporal sequence of the same. Love is all. This shatters our ordinary understanding of cause and causality as we have inherited it from the ancient Greeks, elaborated especially in the writings of Aristotle. See, for example, Gregory of Nazianzus, *Orations,* 42:15, 31:10, and 5:14; and John Zizioulas's discussion in *Communion and Otherness* (London and New York: T&T Clark, 2006), pp. 126-40.

13. Gregory of Nyssa, "On the Soul and the Resurrection," in *Gregory of Nyssa: Dogmatic Treatises, Etc.,* in *A Select Library of the Nicene and Post-Nicene Fathers of the Christian Church,* 2d series, vol. 5 (Grand Rapids: Wm. B. Eerdmans, 1979), pp. 457, 458.

14. David Bentley Hart, *The Beauty of the Infinite* (Grand Rapids: Wm. B. Eerdmans, 2003), p. 274.

15. Athanasius and others employ such speech with the strict meaning. Thus, according to Athanasius, God in his essence is distinct from all creaturely existence, even as in his energies or acts of power, God is in all things. See, for example, *St. Athanasius on the Incarnation,* trans. A Religious C.S.M.V. (Crestwood, N.Y.: St. Vladimir's Seminary Press, 1982), p. 45, par. 17.

16. Kallistos Ware, "Ecological Crisis, Ecological Hope: The Orthodox Vision of Creation," Orthodoxy in America Lecture Series, Fordham University, 5 April 2005, p. 7.

17. The eternity of God's own essence or Triune being must be distinguished, of course, from the derivative or contingent eternity of the world that he eternally destines to exist. We participate in God's eter-

nity *through* his energies that sustain and permeate the Creation. Orthodoxy regards these energies not as a part of God — for the Godhead is simple and indivisible — but as wholly God. As the rays of the sun belong to it, so the energies of God belong to God. Writes Kallistos Ware, "The [divine] essence signifies the whole God as he is in himself" and is utterly transcendent, whereas "the energies signifiy the whole God as he is in his actions" and is truly present to his Creation (*The Orthodox Way*, p. 22).

18. Dumitru Staniloae, *The Experience of God: Orthodox Dogmatic Theology, Volume Two: The World, Creation, and Deification*, trans. Ioan Ionita and Robert Barringer (Brookline, Mass.: Holy Cross Orthodox Press, 2005), p. 14.

19. Alexander Schmemann, *The Journals of Father Alexander Schmemann, 1973-1983*, trans. Juliana Schmemann (Crestwood, N.Y.: St. Vladimir's Seminary Press, 2000), pp. 78, 11.

20. Gregory of Nyssa, *Commentary on the Inscriptions on the Psalms*, p. 28.

21. St. Nicephorus of Constantinople, quoted by Jaroslav Pelikan in *The Melody of Theology: A Philosophical Dictionary* (Cambridge: Harvard University Press, 1988), p. 167.

22. Vladimir Lossky, *Orthodox Theology: An Introduction* (Crestwood, N.Y.: St. Vladimir's Seminary Press, 1978), p. 58.

23. Alexander Schmemann, *The Eucharist* (Crestwood, N.Y.: St. Vladimir's Seminary Press, 1988), p. 75. I thank Chad Marine, a graduate student at the University of Virginia, for pointing out the Lossky and Schmemann passages.

24. *The Festal Menaion*, trans. Mother Mary and Kallistos Ware (London: Faber & Faber, 1977), p. 361.

25. *The Festal Menaion*, p. 378.

26. Alexander Schmemann, *The Church Year*, vol. 2 of *Celebration of Faith* (Crestwood, N.Y.: St. Vladimir's Seminary Press, 1994), p. 64.

27. *Rituale Armenorum: The Administration of the Sacraments and the Breviary Rites of the Armenian Church*, ed. F. C. Conybeare (Oxford: Clarendon Press, 1905), pp. 174-75.

Notes to Pages 19-24

28. *The Festal Menaion,* pp. 354, 355.

29. *Rituale Armenorum,* pp. 169, 170, 171.

30. Increasingly, popular calendars list Sunday as the last day of the week, not the first. This empties Sunday of its Christian significance as the day of Resurrection. The week itself no longer points toward a New Day and a New Creation, only toward a weekend whose exhaustion introduces another secular workweek.

31. St. Gregory of Nazianzus, quoted by Jean Danielou, S.J., in *The Bible and the Liturgy* (Notre Dame, Ind.: University of Notre Dame Press, 1965), p. 269.

32. Thomas Sunday commemorates the doubting apostle's test of the reality of the bodily resurrection of Jesus (John 20:24-29). The Armenian Church remembers this Gospel story on the Sunday after Easter, but the reading is not so central, except insofar as it recalls (and affirms) the Easter event.

33. On day one, in controversy with the Jewish authorities, John the Baptist witnesses to the Christ who comes after him, "whose sandal strap I am not worthy to loose" (John 1:27, NKJV). On day two, John publicly presents Jesus as "the Lamb of God who takes away the sin of the world" (John 1:29, NKJV). On day three, Andrew and an unnamed disciple hear Jesus and follow him (John 1:35-40). On day four, Simon Peter is brought to Jesus (John 1:41-42). On day five, Jesus calls Philip, followed by Nathaniel, both of whom recognize Jesus to be the Messiah and Son of God (John 1:45-51). "On the third day [counting from the call of Philip] there was a wedding in Cana of Galilee . . ." (John 2:1, NKJV). This is day seven. There is no account of happenings on day six.

34. Paul Evdokimov, *The Sacrament of Love* (Crestwood, N.Y.: St. Vladimir's Seminary Press, 1985), p. 122.

35. The text of the translation is adapted from an unpublished source. Citations that follow are from the same source.

36. Unpublished translation.

37. *Divine Liturgy of the Armenian Apostolic Orthodox Church* (London: St. Sarkis Church, 1984), p. 97.

38. Unpublished translation.

Notes to Chapter 2

1. John D. Zizioulas, *Being as Communion* (Crestwood, N.Y.: St. Vladimir's Seminary Press), p. 98.

2. This is as the Septuagint version of the Old Testament renders it, hereafter LXX. The psalm is numbered 71.6 in the LXX.

3. Cyril of Jerusalem, Lecture 15:1, *Catechetical Lectures*, in *A Select Library of Nicene and Post-Nicene Fathers of the Christian Church*, 2d series, vol. 7 (Grand Rapids: Wm. B. Eerdmans, 1978), p. 104.

4. Cyril of Jerusalem, Lecture 15:1, *Catechetical Lectures*, p. 104. St. Matthew took the *Benedictus qui venit* from Psalm 118. St. John introduces a Greek equivalent in Revelation 22:20, and St. Paul employs it in 2 Corinthians 16:22.

5. See Geoffrey Wainwright, *Eucharist and Eschatology* (New York: Oxford University Press, 1981), p. 70.

6. The Cherubic Hymn is the song of the angels who glorify the "King of All" as he enters his Kingdom escorted by divine hosts.

7. *Divine Liturgy of the Armenian Apostolic Church*, trans. Tiran Nersoyan, 5th ed. (London: St. Sarkis Church, 1984), p. 65.

8. *Divine Liturgy of the Armenian Apostolic Orthodox Church*, p. 67.

9. *Divine Liturgy of the Armenian Apostolic Orthodox Church*, p. 69. This movement in the Armenian rite is reminiscent of the eschatological significance that the church finds in Christ's entry into Jerusalem on Palm Sunday. The Gospels tell us that as Jesus descended the Mount of Olives toward the gate of the city, the people rejoiced in praise of God: "'Hosanna to the Son of David. Blessed is He who comes in the name of the Lord!'" (Matt. 21:9, NKJV). The Armenian Vespers for Palm Sunday, called *Ternpatzek* (literally, "the opening of the gates"), interprets the events of the day typologically as prophecy and proleptic "happening" of the Second Coming and the Last Judgment. Jesus enters Jerusalem in humility, riding on an ass, and, in fulfillment of Old Testament messianic prophecy, is received as a king (Matt. 21:5; Zech. 9:9; Isa. 62:11). He will return again with unambiguous power and glory, riding "on the clouds of heaven" (Matt. 24:30, NKJV). The Armenian Vespers juxta-

Notes to Pages 32-39

poses Matthew 21:1-10 and Matthew 24:27-35. The former is Matthew's account of Jesus' entry into Jerusalem, and the latter is his version of the New Testament "small apocalypse." The principal hymn of the Vespers service sets out the eschatological vision: "Grant us, Lord, vigilance with the virgins .../When thou shall come in the glory of Thy Father, to judge the whole world, grant to us to stand on thy right hand,/ That the door of mercy of the heavenly Bridegroom may be opened unto us .../That we may be ready to meet the Bridegroom, and that we may enter the nuptial abode ..." (Amy Apcar, *Melodies of the Five Offices of the Holy Week According to the Holy Apostolic Church of Armenia* [Leipzig: Breitkopf and Haertel, 1902], p. 74). I also detect here an octave of sorts. For the eighth day after Palm Sunday is, of course, Easter Sunday, which confirms that Jesus is Lord.

10. Alexander Schmemann, *Introduction to Liturgical Theology*, trans. Asheleigh E. Moorhouse (New York: St. Vladimir's Seminary Press, 1975), p. 57.

11. *Divine Liturgy of the Armenian Apostolic Orthodox Church*, p. 71.

12. Alexander Schmemann, *For the Life of the World* (Crestwood, N.Y.: St. Vladimir's Seminary Press, 1973), p. 37.

13. *Divine Liturgy of the Armenian Apostolic Orthodox Church*, p. 79.

14. Paul Evdokimov, *In the World, of the World: A Paul Evdokimov Reader*, ed. and trans. Michael Plekon and Alexis Vinogradov (Crestwood, N.Y: St. Vladimir's Seminary Press, 2001), p. 51.

15. Zizioulas, *Being as Communion*, p. 112.

16. *Divine Liturgy of the Armenian Apostolic Orthodox Church*, p. 101.

17. Schmemann, *Introduction to Liturgical Theology*, p. 58.

18. Basil of Caesarea, Homily 2:7 of *The Hexaemeron*, as translated and cited by Schmemann, *Liturgical Theology*, p. 62.

19. Sergius Bulgakov, *The Bride of the Lamb*, trans. Boris Jakim (Grand Rapids: Wm. B. Eerdmans, 2002), p. 385, p. 344.

20. Irenaeus of Lyons, *Against Heresies*, Book 5.35.2, in *Irenaeus of Lyons*, trans. and ed. Robert M. Grant, in the series *The Early Church Fathers* (London and New York: Routledge, 1997), p. 184.

21. Evdokimov, *In the World, of the World: A Paul Evdokimov Reader*, p. 25.

Notes to Chapter 3

1. See Vladimir Lossky, *In the Image and Likeness of God* (Crestwood, N.Y.: St. Vladimir's Seminary Press, 1974), p. 100.

2. Ephrem, Hymn 35, translated and cited by Sebastian Brock in the introduction to Ephrem's *Hymns on Paradise* (Crestwood, N.Y.: St. Vladimir's Seminary Press, 1990), p. 46.

3. The divine name "the Father, the Son, and the Holy Spirit" is not a figure of speech put on and put off by the divine Word during his temporal incarnation. St. Ephrem and the Orthodox tradition are in agreement on this. Rather, the Father, the Son, and the Holy Spirit *is* the immanent relation and identity of the persons as God. The divine name connotes the eternal, transcendent, and hidden coinherence of the three (multiplicity) in one (unity) divinity.

4. Gregory of Nazianzus, "The Second Oration on Easter," in *A Select Library of the Nicene and Post-Nicene Fathers of the Christian Church*, vol. 7 (Grand Rapids: Wm. B. Eerdmans, 1978), p. 431.

5. Lossky, *In the Image and Likeness of God*, p. 101.

6. Cataphatic theology is contrasted to theology that is apophatic. *Apophatic* literally means "negative." By respecting the divine mystery and "unspeakableness" (unfathomable character) of divine life and grace, apophatic or negative theology checks the pretensions of theological literalism and rationalism to be able to affirm clear truths about God, insisting that, for every positive statement about God, there exists a negation that is equally true. For example, while cataphatic theology can assert that "God is good," apophatic theology would insist that "God is not good." Both are correct, but in different ways. As the very principle of goodness underlying all the created goods that we know and to which we usually refer in using the word *good*, God can be called good, or supreme good. But, as a divine Being wholly other than all the

created beings we encounter in daily life, God's goodness is of a very different and (for us) unfathomable order from the created, temporal goods that we know and that provide us with our understanding of the concept "good," which we can apply only by analogy to describe God. This apophaticism is no mere negativism. Rather, because it is respectful of God's transcendence of such categories of good or just, it requires that theology itself transcend the opposites of positive versus negative, or knowledge versus ignorance.

7. Georges Florovksy, *The Collected Works of Georges Florovsky*, vol. 3: *Creation and Redemption* (Belmont, Mass.: Nordland, 1974), pp. 132, 103.

8. Gregory of Nazianzus, "The Second Oration on Easter," p. 433.

9. Sergius Bulgakov, *A Bulgakov Anthology*, ed. James Pain and Nicholas Zernov (Philadelphia: Westminster Press, 1976), p. 170.

10. Cited in *David Anhaght: The "Invincible" Philosopher*, ed. Avedis Sanjian (Atlanta: Scholars Press, 1986), p. 87.

11. Gregory of Nazianzus, "The Second Oration on Easter," p. 433.

12. Cyril of Jerusalem, "First Catechetical Lecture," in *A Select Library of the Nicene and Post-Nicene Fathers of the Christian Church*, vol. 7 (Grand Rapids: Wm. B. Eerdmans, 1978), p. 8.

13. Paul Evdokimov, *Ages of the Spiritual Life* (Crestwood, N.Y.: St. Vladimir's Seminary Press, 1998), pp. 184-85.

14. Athanasius, *St. Athanasius on the Incarnation*, trans. and ed. by a Religious of C.S.M.V. (Crestwood, N.Y.: St. Vladimir's Seminary Press, 1982), p. 41.

15. Ignatius of Antioch, "The Letter to the Ephesians," 7.2, in *The Apostolic Fathers*, ed. Michael W. Holmes (Grand Rapids: Baker, 1999), p. 141.

16. Ambrose, "Exposition of the Gospel of Luke 5:12-13," cited in *Ancient Christian Commentary*, vol. 3: *New Testament: Luke*, ed. Arthur A. Just Jr. (Downers Grove, Ill.: InterVarsity, 2003), pp. 92-93.

17. Irenaeus, *Against the Heresies*, 5.13.1, in *The Ante-Nicene Fathers*, vol. 1 (Grand Rapids: Wm. B. Eerdmans, 1996), p. 539.

18. Gregory of Nyssa, *The Great Catechism*, ch. 15, in *A Select Library*

of the *Nicene and Post-Nicene Fathers of the Christian Church*, vol. 5 (Grand Rapids: Wm. B. Eerdmans, 1979), p. 487.

19. Hymn 8 in "Hymns on the Nativity," in *Ephrem the Syrian: Hymns*, trans. Kathleen E. McVey (New York/Mahwah, N.J.: Paulist Press, 1989), p. 119.

20. "East Coker," Part 2 of *Four Quartets*, IV, lines 7, 10, 21-22 (written in 1940). Available online at www.tristan.icom43.net/quartets/coker.html (23 March 2009).

21. Nicholas Cabasilas, *The Life in Christ* (Crestwood, N.Y.: St. Vladimir's Seminary Press, 1974), pp. 94, 59.

22. Florovsky, *Creation and Redemption*, p. 37.

Notes to Chapter 4

1. Vladimir Lossky, *In the Image and Likeness of God* (Crestwood, N.Y.: St. Vladimir's Seminary Press, 1974), p. 202.

2. G. K. Chesterton, *The Napoleon of Notting Hill*, vol. 6 of *The Collected Works of G. K. Chesterton*, ed. Denis J. Conlon (San Francisco: Ignatius Press, 1991), p. 220.

3. "Tradition says that, to fulfill the prophecy of Joel (Joel 2:28-29), the Holy Spirit descended not only on the twelve chosen Apostles, but also upon all who were with them 'with one accord in one place' (Acts 2:1) ..., that is, on the whole Church. That is why [in] the icon there are represented Apostles not belonging to the twelve — Apostle Paul (sitting with Apostle Peter at the head of the circle of Apostles), and among the seventy, Luke the Evangelist . . . and Mark the Evangelist." Quoted from Leonid Ouspensky and Vladimir Lossky, *The Meaning of Icons* (Crestwood, N.Y.: St. Vladimir's Seminary Press, 1983), p. 208.

4. Michael Quinot, *The Resurrection and the Icon* (Crestwood, N.Y.: St. Vladimir's Seminary Press, 1997), p. 190.

5. Quinot, *The Resurrection and the Icon*, p. 183.

6. Sergius Bulgakov, *The Burning Bush*, in *A Bulgakov Anthology*, ed.

Notes to Pages 72-86

James Pain and Nicholas Zernov (Great Britain: SPCK, 1976; Philadelphia: Westminster Press, 1976), p. 96.

7. Paul Evdokimov, *Woman and the Salvation of the World* (Crestwood, N.Y.: St. Vladimir's Seminary Press, 1994), p. 194.

8. Cabasilas, quoted by Lossky, *In the Image and Likeness of God*, p. 202.

9. Lossky, *In the Image and Likeness of God*, pp. 206-7.

10. Ephrem, Hymn 16.1 in "Hymns on the Nativity," in *Ephrem the Syrian: Hymns*, trans. Kathleen E. McVey (New York/Mahwah, N.J.: Paulist Press, 1989), p. 150.

11. Lossky, *In the Image and Likeness of God*, p. 207.

12. Irenaeus, *St. Irenaeus: Proof of the Apostolic Preaching*, Ancient Christian Writers series, no. 16 (Mahwah, N.J.: Paulist Press, 1952), chap. 33, p. 69.

13. Jacob of Serug, *On the Mother of God* (Crestwood, N.Y.: St. Vladimir's Seminary Press, 1998), Homily 1, p. 25.

14. Alexander Schmemann, *The Virgin Mary*, Celebration of Faith series, vol. 3 (Crestwood, N.Y.: St. Vladimir's Seminary Press, 1995), p. 53.

15. Schmemann, *The Virgin Mary*, p. 53.

16. *The Festal Menaion*, trans. Mother Mary and Kallistos Ware (London: Faber & Faber, 1977), p. 438.

17. Evdokimov, *Woman and the Salvation of the World*, p. 194.

18. St. Cyril of Alexandria, quoted by Evdokimov in *Woman and the Salvation of the World*, p. 196.

19. *Festal Menaion*, pp. 437, 440, 449, 450, 452, 453.

20. Jacob of Serug, *On the Mother of God*, Homily 1, p. 32.

21. Lossky, *In the Image and Likeness of God*, pp. 197-98.

22. Jacob of Serug, *On the Mother of God*, Homily 1, p. 35.

23. Jacob of Serug, *On the Mother of God*, Homily 1, p. 26.

24. Jacob of Serug, *On the Mother of God*, Homily 1, p. 36.

25. Jacob of Serug, *On the Mother of God*, Homily 1, p. 38.

26. Jacob of Serug, *On the Mother of God*, Homily 1, p. 38.

27. Entreaty at Great Vespers, in *The Pentecostarion* (Boston, Mass.: Holy Transfiguration Monastery, 1990), p. 327.

28. Origen, quoted in Luigi Gambero, *Mary and the Fathers of the Church: The Blessed Virgin in Patristic Thought* (San Francisco: Ignatius Press, 1999), pp. 77-78.

29. Romanos, *On the Life of Christ: Kontakia*, trans. Ephrem Lash (San Francisco: HarperCollins, 1995), p. 32.

30. Paul Evdokimov, *The Art of the Icon: A Theology of Beauty* (Redondo Beach, Calif.: Oakwood Publications, 1990), pp. 256-66.

31. The Armenian Midday Hymn for the Feast of the Annunciation, in *The Divine Liturgy of the Armenian Apostolic Orthodox Church*, trans. Tiran Nersoyan, 5th ed. (London: St. Sarkis Church, 1984), pp. 146-47.

Notes to Chapter 5

1. Cyril of Jerusalem, *Catechetical Lectures*, Lecture 13:4, in *A Select Library of the Nicene and Post-Nicene Fathers of the Christian Church*, 2d series, vol. 7 (Grand Rapids: Wm. B. Eerdmans, 1978), p. 83.

2. Georges Florovsky, *Creation and Redemption*, vol. 3 in *The Collected Works of Georges Florovsky* (Belmont, Mass.: Nordland, 1976), p. 110.

3. Florovsky, *Creation and Redemption*, p. 100.

4. *The Teaching of Saint Gregory*, trans. Robert W. Thomson (Cambridge, Mass.: Harvard University Press, 1970), p. 109, par. 477, 488.

5. Dumitru Staniloae, *Theology and the Church*, trans. Robert Barringer (Crestwood, N.Y.: St. Vladimir's Seminary Press, 1980), p. 195.

6. Florovsky, *Creation and Redemption*, p. 136.

7. David Anhaght, "An Encomium on the Holy Cross of God," in *David Anhaght: The "Invincible" Philosopher*, ed. Avedis K. Sanjian (Atlanta, Ga.: Scholars Press, 1986), p. 87.

8. Anhaght, "An Encomium on the Holy Cross of God," p. 85.

9. Paul Evdokimov, *The Art of the Icon: A Theology of Beauty* (Redondo Beach, Calif.: Oakwood Publications, 1990), pp. 133, 314.

Notes to Pages 103-7

10. Leonid Ouspensky and Vladimir Lossky, *The Meaning of the Icon* (Crestwood, N.Y.: St. Vladimir's Seminary Press, 1989), p. 36.

11. Medieval Armenian iconographers may well have clung to it in support of their church's opposition to the two natures Christology of the Council of Chalcedon (451) that both the Byzantine and Roman churches embraced. The Armenian Church favored the "one nature" Christology of St. Cyril of Alexandria (378 44). Cyril defined the unity of divine and human activity in Christ with the formula "One Nature *(mia physis)* of the Word of God incarnate." He employed *physis* in the sense of a concrete reality or being, rather than an abstract set of natural properties that might be described as a "human nature" or a "divine nature." The Armenian Church adheres to this Cyrillian "monophysitism" and affirms that, through an act of divine economy, the preexistent Word of God voluntarily and forever took upon himself (assumed) and enacted the fullness of our humanity. Furthermore, the *Christus Triumphans* style was more compatible with the Armenian Church's leanings toward a strong view of the incorruptibility of Christ's flesh in life, as well as in death.

12. Armenian Canon for the Elevation of the Holy Cross, First Day, in Michael Daniel Findykian, "Armenian Hymns of the Church and Cross," *St. Nersess Theological Review* 11 (2006): 77.

13. Anhaght, "An Encomium on the Holy Cross of God," pp. 85, 87.

14. Armenian Canon for the Elevation of the Holy Cross, First Day, in Findykian, "Armenian Hymns of the Church and Cross," p. 78.

15. "Faith, Hope, Love, and Forgiveness: Mel Gibson Tackles *Passion* Controversy": An Interview with Diane Sawyer on Prime Time. Available online at http://www.talk.livedaily.com/showthread.php?t=391059 (date posted: 14 Feb. 2004).

16. "'Dude, That Was Graphic': Mel Gibson Talks about *The Passion of the Christ*," by Daniel Neff and Jane Johnson Struck. Available online at http://www.christianitytoday.com/movies/interviews/melgibson .html (date posted: 23 Feb. 2004).

17. *The Apostolic Tradition*, in *The Springtime of the Liturgy*, ed. Lucien Deiss (Collegeville, Minn.: Liturgical Press, 1979), pp. 130-31.

18. The Isenheim Altarpiece has two sets of wings that include, among other images, an Annunciation and a Resurrection. The Resurrection is a surreal image with a luminous Christ figure ascending into the night from his tomb in view of his disciples, who, together with the soldiers, are falling to the ground in awe or fear. No doubt this was how Grünewald intended to depict the glory of God in Christ and his final victory over death. But there is no continuity between these two images of Christ on the Cross and Christ flying from the grave. They have not the slightest resemblance to one another. It is as if they are two entirely different beings. This represents a rupture of reality that seems peculiarly modern, a dualism of natural and supernatural that does not belong to traditional iconography.

19. "A Savior's Pain": An Interview by John Baily. Available online at http://www.theasc.com/magazine.mar04/cover/index.html.

20. Gibson also makes his own myth of the Resurrection. Nowhere in the New Testament is the Resurrection described *sans* witnesses at the empty tomb. Nowhere in the Gospels or the Epistles is the actual "event" of the Resurrection described. Yet in *The Passion,* Gibson does just these things. With his "hidden" camera he records the mystery itself: Christ arising from death before the first witnesses have arrived. Though this freedom may be granted the moviemaker, and though this is not the first time an artist has done this, the canons of traditional Christian iconography forbid it.

21. Flannery O'Connor, *Mystery and Manners* (New York: Farrar, Straus & Giroux, 1990), pp. 176, 148.

22. Dante, *Inferno,* 9:61-63.

Notes to Chapter 6

1. *The Lenten Triodion,* trans. Mother Mary and Kallistos Ware (London: Faber & Faber, 1978), p. 656.

2. Ephrem, Hymn 4 in "Hymns on the Nativity," in *Ephrem the Syrian: Hymns,* trans. Kathleen E. McVey (New York/Mahwah, N.J.: Paulist Press, 1989), p. 92.

3. John Chrysostom, Homily 40, in *The Homilies of St. John Chrysostom on the First Epistle to the Corinthians*, Part 2, Library of Fathers of the Holy Catholic Church (Oxford: John Henry Parker; London: J. G. F. and J. Rivington, 1839), p. 572.

4. This manuscript was written and illustrated at the monastery of Gamaghiel at Khizan and is dated 1455. It is owned by the Walters Art Gallery in Baltimore, Maryland.

5. *Rituale Armenorum: The Administration of the Sacrament and Breviary Rites of the Armenian Church*, ed. F. C. Conybeare (Oxford: Clarendon Press, 1905), pp. 168-69.

6. Armenian Canon for the Elevation of the Cross, Second Day, in Michael Daniel Findykian, "Armenian Hymns of the Church and Cross," *St. Nersess Theological Review* 11 (2006): 83.

7. Georges Florovsky, *Creation and Redemption*, vol. 3 of *The Collected Works of Georges Florovsky* (Belmont, Mass.: Nordland, 1976), p. 142.

8. Variables for the Principal Feast Days, in *Divine Liturgy of the Armenian Apostolic Orthodox Church*, trans. Tiran Nersoyan, 5th ed. (London: St. Sarkis Church, 1984), pp. 141-42. The Melodies belong also to Easter Day and Eastertide.

9. Alexander Schmemann, *The Celebration of Faith: Sermons*, vol. 1 (Crestwood, N.Y.: St. Vladimir's Seminary Press, 1991), p. 86.

10. Schmemann, *The Celebration of Faith*, p. 88.

11. *The Lenten Triodion*, p. 622.

12. *The Lenten Triodion*, p. 651.

13. John Chrysostom, Homily 39, in *The Homilies of St. John Chrysostom on the First Epistle to the Corinthians*, p. 562.

14. Schmemann, *The Celebration of Faith*, p. 90.

15. Florovsky, *Creation and Redemption*, p. 141.

16. Here we need to note that Hades is not the same as the hell of suffering and torment that would be inhabited by unrepentant sinners. The latter is a function or consequence of the Incarnation and the Resurrection. It is only with respect to Christ's birth, death, and resurrection — in other words, God's work of redemption in and through his only begotten Son — that Hell as a "state" of "eternal" reprobation of the

unrepentant is possible. Only with the judgment that Christ brings is the wheat winnowed, the chaff separated from it (Matt. 3:12).

17. Florovsky, *Creation and Redemption*, p. 139.

18. The doctrine concerning the union of the divine Logos and human nature in Jesus Christ that St. Cyril of Alexandria (398-444) propounded in its most profound form was the standard for the Christological teaching of the Councils of Ephesus (431) and Chalcedon (451). It states that the divine Logos is the sole personal subject of the Incarnation. Jesus Christ is the pre-existent Son of God who has taken the whole of our humanity into his being. The Hypostatic Union, therefore, means that the fullness of divinity and the fullness of humanity are united in the Person of Christ.

19. Gregory of Nyssa, "The Great Catechism," in *A Select Library of Nicene and Post-Nicene Fathers of the Christian Church*, 2d series, vol. 5 (Grand Rapids: Wm. B. Eerdmans, 1979), p. 489.

20. John of Damascus, "An Exact Exposition on the Orthodox Faith," book 3, ch. 27, in *A Select Library of the Nicene and Post-Nicene Fathers of the Christian Church*, vol. 11 (Grand Rapids: Wm. B. Eerdmans, 1989), p. 72. "Topically" could be translated as "spatially," but this is confusing because the separation does not conform to our ordinary conceptions of space or time.

21. *Service Book of the Holy Orthodox-Catholic Apostolic Church*, ed. and trans. Isabel Florence Hapgood (Englewood, N.J.: Antiochian Orthodox Christian Archdiocese, 1975), p. 237.

22. Paul Evdokimov, *The Art of the Icon: A Theology of Beauty* (Redondo Beach, Calif.: Oakwood Publications, 1990), p. 325.

23. Nicholas Berdyaev, *The Destiny of Man* (New York: Harper & Row, 1960), p. 294.

24. *Rituale Armenorum*, p. 121.

25. *The Lenten Triodion*, pp. 625, 627.

26. *Service Book of the Holy Orthodox-Catholic Apostolic Church*, p. 235.

SUBJECT INDEX

Adam and Eve, 28, 38, 56-57, 76, 85, 119, 120, 124, 134; Adam, 16, 54-55, 94, 105, 128, 135; Eve, 84, 125
Ambrose of Milan, Saint, 58-59
Anhaght, David, 54, 97, 103-4
Annunciation, 67-69, 73-86
Anselm of Canterbury, Saint, 47-51, 93
Aquinas, Thomas, 93
Armenian Earthquake of 1988, 91, 115-18, 132-33
Armenian Liturgy, 30-35, 63, 125-27; burial service, 135; elevation of the Holy Cross, 98, 103, 105, 123-24; Epiphany, 19-20, 121; matins, 5-6; New Sunday, 22-24
Ascension, 27, 69, 86-87, 94
Assumption. *See* Dormition of the Mother of God
Athanasius, Saint, 13, 56
Augustine, Saint, 54, 56, 61

Baptism, 18, 22, 23, 43, 55, 60, 121-25

Barsegh (Plate 5), 100, 103-5
Basil the Great, Saint, 9, 35-36, 45
Berdyaev, Nicholas, 135
Bulgakov, Sergius, 36, 53-54, 71

Cabasilas, Nicholas, 61, 73
Calvin, John, 93
Chesterton, G. K., 67
Cyril of Alexandria, Saint, 80
Cyril of Jerusalem, Saint, 29-30, 43-44, 54, 93, 94, 100, 106

Dante, 6, 112
Dormition of the Mother of God (Assumption), 68, 71-72
Dostoyevsky, Fyodor, 6

Easter, 20-23, 119; Second Easter (New Sunday), 22-24
Eighth Day or Octave, 20-22, 35, 136
Elevation of the Holy Cross, 103, 123-24
Eliot, T. S., 60
Ephrem the Syrian, Saint, 44-45, 60, 74, 83, 120-21, 134

Subject Index

Epiphany, 17-21, 121
Eucharist, 16, 28, 33-35, 39, 60-61, 91, 106, 110, 114, 132
Evdokimov, Paul, 1, 22, 34, 40, 55, 72, 80, 89, 102, 134
Eve. *See* Adam and Eve

Fall, The, 15-16, 56-57, 59-60
Faulkner, William, 10
Florovsky, Georges, 52-53, 62, 95, 124, 131
Freedom: Christ's, 48, 52, 57, 96; God's, 12; human, 112; Mary's, 67, 68, 73, 75-86

Gregory of Nazianzus, Saint, 9, 48-49, 53
Gregory of Nyssa, Saint, 5, 6, 12, 15, 60, 131
Grünewald, Matthias (Figure 4, p. 108), 107-9

Hades, 28, 37-38, 118-19, 121-22, 124, 127, 129-30, 132-35
Hart, David Bentley, 13
Heaven, 6, 23, 27, 28, 41, 120
Hell, 120-23, 136
Holy Friday, 27, 38, 94, 95, 119
Holy Saturday, 27, 37-39, 119-22, 128, 130, 133
Hypostatic Union, 131-32

Icon(s) and iconography, 37, 68, 102, 125, 134; of Annunciation (Plate 3), 81; of Ascension, 69; of Crucifixion (Figure 2, p. 99; Figure 3, p. 101, and Plate 5), 98-105, 107-11, 119; of Descent of the Holy Spirit or Pentecost (Figure 1, p. 70 and Plate 2), 68-71; of Dormition of the Mother of God, 71-72; of Enthroned Theotokos, 90; of Epiphany (Plate 6), 122; of Harrowing of Hades or Anastasis (Plate 1 and Plate 7), 37-39, 122-24, 134; of Myrrh-Bearing Women (Plate 8), 37, 124-25; Nativity, 29; of Our Lady of Vladimir (Plate 4), 89
Ignatius of Antioch, Saint, 57
Image of God, 16, 56-57
Immaculate Conception, 75
Irenaeus of Lyons, Saint, 39, 59, 75-76
Isenheim Altarpiece (Figure 4, p. 108), 107-10

Jacob of Serug, 76-77, 83-86
John Chrysostom, Saint, 121, 129, 136
John the Baptist, Saint, 109-10, 122, 134
John the Evangelist and Apostle, 109, 113

Karenkin I, Catholicos, 90-91
Kenosis, 52, 78, 88, 134
Khatchatur (Plates 2, 6, 7, 8), 69-71, 121-25

Lewis, C. S., 4, 35
Liturgy, 2-4, 15-17, 21, 24, 25-26, 28, 32-33, 39-40; Annunciation, 80, 81-83; Ascension, 86; Compline, 18; Easter, 131-32, 136; Epiphany, 19; Holy Friday, 95; Holy Saturday, 120, 128;

Subject Index

Matins, 18; Vespers, 72. *See also* Armenian Liturgy

Lossky, Vladimir, 16, 49-50, 65, 74, 84

Luke, Saint, 68, 113-14

Luther, Martin, 93

Mary Magdalene, Saint, 109

Moses, 40, 134

Myrrh-Bearing Women (Plate 8), 37, 122, 124-27

New Creation, 10, 16-24, 35, 39-41, 91, 136

O'Connor, Flannery, 111-12

Origen, 87

Palm Sunday, 31

Paul, Saint, 10-11, 28, 36, 40, 50, 52, 55, 62, 65, 68, 78, 94, 98, 117-18, 120, 125, 129, 133, 135

Pentecost, 21, 34-35, 40, 68-75, 120

Peter, Saint, 34, 40-41, 119-20

Rabula Gospel Illuminations (Figure 3, p. 101), 100-103, 105

Satan, 38, 122-24, 135

Schmemann, Father Alexander, 14, 16, 18, 78-79, 127-28, 130

Simeon, Saint, 86-88

Sin, 23, 40, 41, 44, 49, 54-59, 60, 62, 65, 85, 87, 95-96, 103, 120; ancestral sin (original sin), 60

Staniloae, Dumitru, 14, 96

Trinity, 12-14, 15, 16, 131-32

Ware, Metropolitan Kallistos, 9

Zizioulas, Metropolitan John, 28, 34

SCRIPTURE INDEX

OLD TESTAMENT			104:24	13	NEW TESTAMENT	
			104:33	3-4		
Genesis					**Matthew**	
1:2	17		**Wisdom**		5:48	73
1:3-4	3		1:14	10	6:10	27
1:9-10	3				9:1-8	58
1:24-25	3		**Isaiah**		9:12-13	59
1:26	56				12:29	44
3:4	56		6:3	15	18:12-14	44
3:5	56		40:22	2	18:20	27
			55:8	12	21:9	29
Exodus					23:39	29
3:14	28		**Daniel**		24:29ff.	28
			3:19-28	41	28	37
1 Samuel			3:25	41	28:20	27
2:8	2		7:13	28		
					Mark	
Psalms			**Hosea**		1:9-10	17
19(18 LXX):4	31		13:14	119	1:10	18
19(18 LXX):5	31				2:1-12	58
24(23 LXX):7-10	31				2:5	58
68(67 LXX):33	31		**Habakkuk**		2:7	58
72:6	29		3:3	31	2:10	58
74:13-14	123				10:46-52	57-58
104:2	29		**Malachi**		10:52	57
104:5	2		3:10	2	13:24	37, 39

Scripture Index

13:26	28, 37, 39	**Acts**		6:11-12	44
13:32	36	1:11	27		
16	37	2:14-28	37	**Philippians**	
		2:16-17	34	2:2-11	88
Luke		2:31-32	120	2:5-8	52
1:31	67	17:32	62-63	2:5-11	78
1:34	81	17:34	63	4:6	10-11
1:35	73			4:7	10
1:38	68, 75	**Romans**			
1:46-55	66	3:23-25	49	**1 Thessalonians**	
1:49-53	80	3:24-26	44	4:14	33
2:19	68	5:12	55	5:1-2	36
2:34-35	86	6:4	65	5:2	28
2:35	86	8:21	54		
5:17-26	58			**1 Timothy**	
11:21-22	44	**1 Corinthians**		2:6	44
15:4-7	44	1:25	97		
17:21	14	7:31	10, 40	**Hebrews**	
23:43	27	15	117	9:11	16
24	37	15:21-22	55	9:15	44
24:13-35	113	15:26	132	12:2	29
24:22-23	113	15:50	55, 102	13:8	33
24:25-26	105	15:51-54	118		
24:26-27	113	15:52	133	**1 Peter**	
24:30-32	114	15:52-55	57	1:25	10
		15:53	55, 129	3:18-19	37
John		15:55	55, 115	3:19-20	28
1:1-2	22			4:6	119-20
1:2-3	17	**2 Corinthians**			
1:3	22	3:18	57	**2 Peter**	
1:18–2:11	22	13:4	98	1:4	56
1:29	110			3:10	37, 39
2:1-11	22	**Galatians**		3:11	41
3:30	109	3:13	44, 52	3:13	26, 41
6:39	14				
10:1-18	44	**Ephesians**		**1 John**	
19:27	71	4:8-10	120	2:25	56
19:30	112, 113	4:13	57, 68, 80	3:16	97
20	37	4:22-24	68	4:8-10	51

157

Scripture Index

4:16	14	5:9-13	10	21:4	59
		5:12-13	23	21:5	39
Revelation		14:3	41	22:5	10
1:17-18	128-29	19:7	24	22:13	8, 29
5:9	23, 41	19:7-8	22	22:20	27
5:9-10	23	21:1	23		